# 16 Generations of Lybrand's

*From Germany to Charleston, SC to Lexington, SC to Chapin, SC to Pelion, SC to Aiken, SC to Edisto Beach, SC*

1543 - 2004

Sam Lybrand

Printed in the United States of America

ISBN: 9798679276895
10 9 8 7 6 5 4 3 2 1

EMPIRE PUBLISHING
www.empirebookpublishing.com

Note: The front cover has the family name as "Leibbrand". Some material I found spelled the family name as "Leibbrand(t). When the family got to Charleston, SC to receive the Promised Land Grant the English pronounced the "lei" as " Ly". Plus, they had to pledge allegiance to the King of England, therefore the name was changed to "Lybrand".

# Dedications

This book is dedicated to my first wife, Ida Margaret Myers, who I was married to for 40 years. She gave me three wonderful children. She had an untimely death in early 2000 and is truly missed. It is also dedicated to my children, Jimmy, Amy and John and their children. Included in this dedication are my second wife, Joyce Hills Abrams, who I grew up with on Edisto, and her children who have taken me in and treated me so well.

## My Children:

1. **James Samuel Lybrand,** my firstborn, born in Puerto Rico in 1960 while I was in the service. He married **Melinda Jozette Starnes.**
   Their children are **Samuel Dupree Lybrand** and **Laken Jozette Lybrand.**
2. **Amy Margaret King,** my second child. She was born in Orangeburg, SC in 1963 while I was working at my first job out of the service. She married **Matthew King.**
   Their children are **Anne Harley King, James Oliver King** and **Robert David King.**
3. **John Myers Lybrand,** my third child, also born in Orangeburg, SC in 1965 while I was working at my first job. He married **Elizabeth Hay.**
   Their children are **John Daniel Hay Lybrand,** and **Sarah Elizabeth Lybrand.**

## Joyce's Children:

1. **Karen Abrams Peterson,** who is married to **Bill Peterson.**
   Karen's children by her first husband are **Joseph Bradford Smith,** and **Leah Katherine Smith.**
2. **Pamela Abrams Welch,** who is married to **Kyle Welch.**
   Their child is **Garrett Kyle Welch.**
3. **Marie Abrams Asbill,** who is currently not married.

Her Children are **Marsh Seabrook Elliott**, **Tide McTeer Elliot,** and **August Savanna Asbill** from two previous marriages.

**4.** **Joseph Scott Abrams**, who is married to **Josie Shimp**.

Their children are, **Emma Louise Abrams** and **James Lucas Abrams.**

# Credits

The credits listed below are for both Volume One and Volume Two so that I have all those people that helped me in one place.

From the start I want to recognize those who have helped me put these books together and those books or other sources I have used to help put some color and flavor to this book. Without all this help these books would not have been possible. These are not listed in any particular order so that I am not giving anyone special recognition, except for my wife who worked tirelessly to try to help me write this story as clearly as possible. Just know that I sincerely appreciate all the help I have received.

### Individuals that so kindly helped me with this book.

- **Joyce Lybrand,** of Edisto Island, my wife, who has worked tirelessly editing and improving my sentence structure to make these books more readable. Without her this would not have happened. These books would be only a dream of mine without her. Thanks, Joyce.
- **Amy Lybrand King,** of Summerville, SC, my daughter, who saved my family pictures for me to use in these books.
- **David Lybrand,** of Edisto Island, SC, my brother, who provided a story or two and some great pictures of Rockville. He also helped me get pictures of White Shell.
- **Jim Lybrand,** of Pelion, SC., my son. He did some fact gathering for me for this book.
- **Jack Lybrand,** of Columbia, SC, a distant relative, who first sparked my interest in finding out about my ancestry and provided a copy of his own book on the Lybrand's, of which I have used a portion. He also provided additional stories and pictures.
- **Jimmy Lybrand,** of Sally, SC, a distant relative, who provided pictures and stories of my ancestors in the New Holland, SC area.

- **George Marion Lybrand,** of West Columbia, SC, a distant relative, provided a great letter about my father's first real job as a teacher in New Holland, SC.
- **Bobby Lybrand,** of Pelion, SC, a distant relative who told me how to get in touch with his sister, Frances Tyler, who in turn provided great information.
- **LeMyra T. Young,** of Wagener, SC, a distant relative, who provided what I would consider a vast amount of information and pictures that made this book come alive in some places.
- **Frances Tyler,** of Wagener, SC, a distant relative, who provided a nice long letter with her experiences with the Lybrand's.
- **Phil Hydrick,** of August, GA. who told me how to get in touch with Marcia Hydrick Foreman, who provided invaluable information about my grandfather, grandmother and Thelma, my father's older sister.
- **Marcia Hydrick Foreman,** of North August, SC, a cousin, who sent me pictures of my grandfather and grandmother. She also sent me a picture of Daddy's sister Thelma, who I had never seen. Without her a great hole would be left in this book. Thanks again, Marcia.
- **Doris Brittain,** of California, a distant relative who I talked to in 1985 and who sent me a book she had written called **Lybrand Oaks.** I have used some of her material in this book.
- **William B. Rauch,** of Chapin, SC, a distant relative, provided invaluable information about John Lybrand, Sr. and John (Jack) Lybrand, Jr. His family married into the Lybrand clan in the 1800s. Bill is the President of the_**Dutch Fork Chapter of SCGS, Inc.** (South Carolina Genealogy Society)
- **Shirley F. Trotter,** of Lexington, SC, a distant relative, provided letters from and about Wesley Allen

Lybrand and several pictures of my great, great aunts. I have a section inserted called "Shirley's Extra" in volume two that includes all the information she provided. She is also a member of the **Dutch Fork Chapter of the SCGS, Inc.** as the State Representative.

- **Jamie Dalhousie,** 17th Earl of Dalhousie, gave me permission to use the portrait of Governor James Glen who signed Hendrick Lybrand's land grant in 1755. Thanks again, Jamie. What a find.
- **Tide Elliott,** of Edisto Island, SC, Joyce's grandson. He allowed me to take a picture of the mammoth leg bone he found on Edisto.
- **Marie Asbill,** of Edisto Island, SC, Joyce's daughter. She allowed me to take a picture of the mammoth tooth she found on Edisto.
- **Matthew Kizer,** of Edisto Island, SC. He gave me the picture of Deveaux Bank that I have used in this book.
- **Elizabeth M. Johnson,** Deputy State House Preservation Office, SC Department of Archives and History. She gave me permission to use the pictures of Fig Island. Credit for obtaining these pictures goes to The National Register of Historical Places program at the SC Department of Archives of History. I thank them for providing these pictures.
- **Susan Roberts,** of Edisto Island, SC who gave me permission to use her pictures of the Painting Bunting and the Bald Eagles. She is a professional photographer who works out of Edisto. She is a well know photographer and I greatly appreciate her allowing me to use these two beautiful pictures.
- **The Post and Courier,** of Charleston, SC. I have used several old articles that my wife, Joyce, had saved over the years that came from **The Post and Courier.**
- The sunset photograph on the last page was taken by

one of our neighbors when Joyce and I were coming back from fishing in Store Creek. This is a once in a lifetime opportunity when everything came together at a moment in time that may never happen  again.

- **Unknown helper or provider of information.** Being the old man that I am I am sure I have left someone out. Therefore, if you are reading this and contributed something to this book then I also thank you.

# A Special Creation
### (A Sam 's ACE Basin Story.)

A wise old man once told me that after God had rested a day from His six days of creating the Earth, He sat back and thought to Himself, "I need to spend a few days creating something special for many to really see what I can do so it will be protected as something special and enjoyed down throughout the ages." This area was recently rediscovered and named the ACE Basin. I grew up exploring this beautiful area and knew it was special, but did not know how special it was until a few years ago when it began to be taken into a conservation area. It was named for the three rivers flowing through it and terminating in the unique St. Helena Sound. One of these three rivers is called the South Edisto River and is the longest. It originates all the way up in the sand hills of South Carolina. The two other great rivers are called the Combahee and the Ashepoo.

I had the great pleasure of experiencing ·this extraordinary, breathtakingly beautiful place as I grew up right in the middle of it. I could go on forever telling. you about my adventures, but I will start with a recent experience that I think should show off some of the exciting things you can expect to see in the ACE Basin.

My wife and I live on Store Creek, which is one of the longest salt water creeks in the area and has many plantation homes situated on its banks. It used to be one of the main ways to get from place to place on Edisto Island back in the plantation days when Edisto was one of the richest places on the Earth.

One day my wife and I went out fishing in our sixteen-foot johnboat with its 15 hp outboard motor, just perfect for fishing in the local creeks. We anchored close to shore near an old oak tree that had fallen in the water where we had caught spot tail bass before. Shortly after, we had anchored a huge bottlenose dolphin came toward us. He was moving so fast close to the surface of the water that he was throwing a wake in front of him. He was coming toward us so quickly that we became afraid that he would run over us. When he got about 50 feet away from us, he stopped and, with his large tail, knocked a spot 'tail bass up on the bank. He then came out of the water, wiggled up the bank, took the bass in his beak-like jaw, wiggled back into the water and swam off. A few minutes later he came up close to our johnboat with the bass in his mouth and seemed to say, " See, I still have him, can you catch fish like this?" He then swam off, not to be seen again.

This is a short story to whet your appetite as to what you can expect to see when you visit my paradise that God spent two extra days to create. Since I have spent most of my life in this amazing area, I have many other stories and adventures to tell you. Look for them in this publication as each issue is published. Some will be short and others a little longer. Some stories just take a while to tell.

Sam Lybrand

# Introduction

This is a series of two books that need to be read as one. The first volume is about what interest me about Edisto Island and about some of the things I personally did coming up on Edisto. It is not written as a history of Edisto but as a number of facts and unique experiences I have had.

Volume Two contains as much information I could find out about my Lybrand ancestors and how the Lybrand's fit into Edisto Island and its development starting in 1942. The Lybrand's must have left a lasting memory on Edisto because there is a long street on Edisto Beach named after my father. His name was Harvie Samuel Lybrand. At the present time there are still Lybrand's living on Edisto Island and to most people familiar with Edisto it is a recognizable name associated with Edisto.

This introduction is the same in both Volume One and Volume Two.

In my mind's eye Edisto Island is all about the mysteries of life that can be enjoyed on this special place called *"Ed-is-tow"*. Edisto is like a very enjoyable book that you have to read to its end so that your lasting memories will be recalled as warm and wonderful. While reading, if you get emotionally involved and relate to each character or event, it makes the book even more enjoyable. Therefore there is no table of contents for you to be able to pick and choose which chapters or sections you will read.

Have absolutely no doubt, and there is no apology, from the beginning, that these books are about Sam Lybrand and what interests him about Edisto Island and his ancestors. It also has as many pictures as I could take that would show off the character of Edisto and why I have loved it most of my life. Many old family pictures are included. The pictures that were provided by others are clearly identified. I believe that pictures speak thousands of words at one glance. Therefore you might call these books picture books.

As stated above, this book is in two volumes. Volume One has a few pictures, taken by me, of scenes that I think represent Edisto in living color. I am not a professional photographer; I just used a good camera and all I had to do was get the sun right and then push one button. The second section in Volume One is also about what interests me about Edisto and things I did or experienced while living on Edisto as a young child and a teenager as far back as I can remember. I have included a little about my college experience and my early military experience. Keep in mind that I am 75 years old while writing this and some things may be out of the order in which they happened.

Volume Two is about my early life while living in Aiken, SC and includes much about my parents. I have researched and written down all I could find out about my direct family line. This search took me back to 1542 in Germany and goes up to the present. Sixteen generations of Lybrand's directly related to me are included. It took my family 13 generations to finally settle on my paradise called Edisto Island.

Therefore if you want to get the complete Sam Lybrand *Edisto* story you need to read both volumes.

Also, as a disclosure, I am not well versed in the English language and I am told I write in conversational English. But most people understand what I say when I say it. So please excuse any misuse of the King's English. My wife, Joyce, has edited this book the best she could. I overrode her many times because I liked the way I said some things better than the way she thought I should have said them. I have received several letters and comments from other people, mostly distant relatives and have recorded what they wrote as they wrote them just to keep the flavor of their writings and how they told their stories, etc.

The pictures I present in Volume One are to let you begin to see what you can expect to see and enjoy on Edisto. But I must warn you that you will not see Edisto in all its beauty unless you get off the main drag. Take a tour or two and read some of the great books written about Edisto and then go seek out the interesting places on Edisto.

In Volume One I have put small explanations in boxes on each picture to wet your whistle as to what my sea island paradise has to offer. As my Edisto story unfolds, with the flavor of the Lybrand influence inserted, the Edisto experience will reveal itself to those who seek its peace and tranquility. As I put these books together I realized more and more how fortunate I am to have lived on such a place which God took an extra measure to create. As I have said before this is not a history book. It is about what interests me and some stories of what I have experienced over the past three quarters of a century. Come join with me as I try to reveal what interests me about "Edisto". If you read these two books and have not visited Edisto Island, you will come! Many come and never go home.

I believe God created everything and nothing on earth just happened by chance. Therefore from time to time you will see Bible verses here and there. While doing my research on my part of the Lybrand clan I was struck by how often God and the Bible came up either directly or indirectly by the actions of many of my ancestors.

As you read through these books and start enjoying all the pictures and stories, you will begin to understand why I wrote these books. From the start it was my desire to leave a written record of my youth and what I did and experienced over my life so that my children and grandchildren and maybe great-grandchildren will know what their grandfather was like and what he liked to do with his time here on God's green Earth.

It is my earnest desire that my descendants keep records of the special events in their lives and write a book that will continue where these books left off. It would be special if, after several more generations, my descendants could read all about who came before them and some of their life experiences. This book may give others the same idea and they could leave such a book for their descendants.

God bless all that read this book, every one of you! Granddaddy Sam

*"In the beginning was the Word, and the Word was with God, and the Word was God. The same was in the beginning with God."*

*"All things were made by Him; and without Him was not anything made that was made. In Him was life; and the life was the light of men."*
John 1:1-4 KJV

# Comments

One thing that became evident while doing this research was that for the most part the Lybrand clan were and are a religious group. The first group that came over were referred to as German Lutherans. They built a church that is now under the water of Lake Murray. It was referred to as the Lybrand Lutheran Church. Sometime around the Civil War my line moved to the Pelion/New Holland area and became Methodist. My great grandfather gave the land and lumber to build a church in the area. When we moved to Edisto Beach in 1947 our family joined the Presbyterian Church.

Note, this book was written after my first book about my childhood coming up on Edisto Beach, SC, titled, **Sam's Edisto Island Paradise.** This first book is published and is on Amazon to be purchased by anyone that is interested. This book shows how we got to Edisto Beach with all the generation before as far as I could find out. To my surprise I was able to go back to 1542. I was also surprised to find that in the 16 generation all had a male Lybrand which made it easier to put my genealogy together. Another thing that I found was that there were five Sam's in a row without a junior. For example, they were **John Samuel Lybrand, Harvey Samuel Lybrand, George Samuel Lybrand** (Me), **James Samuel Lybrand** (My son), and **Samuel Dupree Lybrand** (His son).

The way I was able to put this genealogy together was that I went to the white pages where I thought most of the Lybrand's lived and wrote every Lybrand I could find and ask them what they knew about the ancestry of the Lybrand's. I put a self-addressed stamped envelope with each letter to make it easy for them to reply. Some came back and said that they knew nothing and did not care. Some came back with a large section of my ancestry. Some referred me to other relatives that that might have information I could use. Several had written small books with their personal genealogy of their family and sent me a copy. Of course, I followed up on these referrals. This book is the result of everything I received over a two-year period.

I only followed the male Lybrand's that I was directly related too. If I had traced all my grandmothers, I'd still be doing this research. I found that if you follow all that you can claim kin you could spend years.

My research uncovered information on Mother's side, but not as much as I found on my father's side. So, I included this information. Surprising both of my great, great grandfathers were in the Civil War and both about died as a result of serving in the terrible war.

I met many other Lybrand's. What was interesting was that all the people I talked to with Lybrand as their last name came from Hendrick Lybrand who is the one that came to Charleston, SC in 1753 and received a Land Grand in what we now call **The Midlands of South Carolina.**

While I was doing this research, several people called and said, "Are we kin?" One lady from Johns Island called and we found that she came from one of the sons of the second generation that came to Charleston, SC in 1753. My son what lives in Summerville, SC told me

# Just in Case

In case you miss it, this genealogy was originally researched and printed for my children and grandchildren.

I have had so much interest in this that I decided to have it published and put on amazon so many people can enjoy it.

Therefore, the dates may seem a little strange because I finished my research a while back and now, I am having it published. I was around 75 years old when much of this was done. Now I am 83 years old.

So just consider that I am and old storyteller and enjoy all that I found out about my ancestry.

I was very pleased about all that I was able to find out about those that came before me. Many that have read this material were surprised and jealous about all that it includes.

I hope you enjoy it. I was saddened when I had gone back as far as I could because I enjoyed reading about those that came before me.

# How Did I Get Here?

Did you personally do anything to cause your presence here on this beautiful earth?

Have you given any thought to what your gene pool is made of!

Do you know anything about what your ancestors went through to live long enough to have children? How did the generations continue until it became your time to be born?

Why do you call the place you are living Home? Who decided that you should live where you are living?

Who determined what kind of education you now have?

Why do you believe in God and how do you worship God? Do you stand up and clap during a service or do you quietly sit back and take it all in and are inspired by the glory of God?

How about the color of your skin and how you talk? Did you have anything to do with the color of your skin and how you talk?

How about your friends, husband or wife? How did you meet them and why did you meet them?

Who determined what talents you have and why you don't know how to do some things?

Why are you living at your current age when so many have died much younger than you?

Why do you have children or not have children?

We are all given a life to live and it is not what happens to you or who your ancestors were. Your contentment and contribution to life here on earth is what you do with the hand you are dealt.

It is nice to know where you came from as this book will tell you. But the good news is that tomorrow is the rest of your life and how you spend it will be up to you.

How about writing down the special events of your life so that your descendants will know about the life you lived?

# Lybrand
## Introduction

In this volume I will try to give my children and grandchildren a bit of their heritage. Chapter One will deal with my life as told talking about my father and myself.

Chapter Two will deal with my father's brother and sisters and what I know about my mother's family.

Chapter Three will deal with my direct line as far as I was able to go back in time. It will also include all the personal stories and events that happened to my ancestors that I could find. It is my hope that after reading all that I have found out about my ancestors that they will come alive and not just be a name, when they were born and when they died. This chapter is about the dash between the date they were born and the date they died. Several close and distant relatives have contributed to this chapter. At the beginning of any material I received from a relative I identify the person who gave it to me in order to give him or her full credit. If they provided a picture I have identified the one that provided it. This has been a long process over several years of following leads on who may have information on a particular ancestor. I said several years, but it actually started when I moved to Columbia in 1969 and began to see all the Lybrand names. Some even belonged to blacks that I became acquainted with. They even called me "cousin". As you will see, some Lybrand's owned a few slaves which are named in this book. Over the years I found out this and that and did some writing. But when I retired from full time real estate sales in April of 2011, I began in earnest putting all that I had found out about the Lybrand's in this book.

As I write this book I have tried to insert what being a Christian means to me. I hope that my children and grandchildren will come to understand that they are on this earth for a short time and will spend eternity either in heaven or in hell. Let me tell you right here and now that you don't want to spend eternity in hell. Where you spend eternity is up to us. Read John 3:18 in the Holy Bible and ponder what it actually means. Your reaction toward this will determine your future.

What I hope that you take away from this book is that the Lybrand's have always been hard working and God-fearing people from as far back as I can find. The Lybrand family goes back far into European history and also helped settle America from its beginning. Therefore, if you have the last name of Lybrand or are directly kin to the Lybrand's you can hold your head high as coming from a well-established and honorable people. One of my proud moments was when I realized that my direct ancestors, including me, helped form four Christian churches. As a result I may mention this again as this story develops.

It is my hope that some of my children and grandchildren will continue where I left off and continue a history of the Sam Lybrand family for generations to come. Then in time to come all of my descendants will have clear and interesting information about who went before them and maybe learn a little about the dos and don'ts of life.

God bless you all, every one of you.

# Father and Son

Since the first chapter starts off talking about my father, Harvie S. Lybrand, and me, I thought it appropriate to start with a few pictures of my father and me plus the Lybrand coat-of-arms. I believe one picture can tell more than a thousand words. Therefore, as you have noticed, I have included as many pictures as I could fit into this book.

Daddy before we moved to Edisto in 1947

Me before we moved to Edisto

Me just before Daddy demanded I get a boy's haircut.

# Chapter One

My Grandchildren, in this chapter, I am going to try to tell you what I can remember about coming up in Aiken, SC, before we moved to Edisto in 1947. This will be done through talking about my father and myself. As stated in my introduction to this section, I will talk about other members of my family. After I finish this, I will try to tell you all I know about my direct line of the Lybrand Clan. I am not going to try to follow all the other relatives that I could follow because it would take a lifetime. But if you want to follow any of the other lines, there is enough information in this book to give you a starting point.

I was born in the Aiken County Hospital on April 3, 1937. My mother was Jennie Owens Lybrand, and my father was Harvie Samuel Lybrand. I was the second of three boys. Thomas Harvie Lybrand and David Ladson Lybrand were my brothers. Tommy was four years older, and David was four years younger. My full name is George Samuel Lybrand, but I have always been called Sammie or Sam all my life. (My grandfather was called Sammie also. I understand that I also inherited his personality.) I often call myself Sambolie because Sam is the second most common dog name, and Sambo is now considered racist. As you probably have already figured out, life is sometimes very funny to me because of the way people take things and make a mountain out of a molehill. People that have known me as a youth call me Sammie. From college on, I was called Sam. My father told me that his father was called Sammie and that is why they called me Sammie from my birth.

In thinking about what order I should tell this story, I began to think that what I have done in my life started with what I first learned from my father and mother. Therefore I will begin this story with what I know or have learned about and from my Daddy. I seldom think of him as my father. And of course, I will include some things I learned from my mother. I will probably tell you this again: the loneliest day of my life was when my mother died. She was the only one that did things "just because."

Along our journey of life, we all come to decision points that determine the rest of our lives. Look for these decisions as I go along. These points are what kind of education you seek, what kind of job you have, who you marry, where you decide to live, and other such decisions. Some things happen to you that affect the rest of your life, such as having no control over who your parents are and where you are born. Other such events are the untimely deaths of people in your immediate family. When these events happen, what really will affect your life is how you deal with them. Some people I have seen over my lifetime, just lose it, and others just take what is handed to them and deal with it the best they can. Therefore when these changes come up in your life, seek God's wisdom and then go on with your life. The best example of how not to deal with a death is the death of Little Milton, Uncle Milton's, and Aunt Vera's son who died at age 10. They really never got over his death and died as sad old people. I am not saying that the death of a loved one, especially a child, is not a sad event. I am suggesting that we all die. Some die young, and some live to an old age. Death is a part of living. We all die and hopefully go to a better place. Therefore after a grieving period, we must all get on living our lives as best we can.

One of the things that I learned while working for General Electric in Hendersonville, NC, was what they required of all their salaried people. It goes like this, "Make a decision, knowingly if you can, ignorantly if you must, but make a decision and never fear the consequences." By making prompt decisions based on the best information available, you will probably not be too far off. Once you have made a decision, you will find out how good a decision you made and if there are any flaws, you can take corrective actions. But if you never make a decision, you will never get anywhere, and life will just happen to you without your own input. This decision-making process has served me well.

# Harvie Samuel Lybrand
**August 2, 1904 - November 25, 1997**
*(I hope this section puts a little life into the dash on his tombstone.)*

Any story about one's life must include something about his father, if he had one in his life to influence him and his future thinking. One is fortunate when he has a father that lives with him. In our current society this is sadly not always the case and our whole nation is suffering because of the lack of righteous fathers in our homes. Therefore, let me talk about my Daddy for a while. Most of this information I remember personally but some was handed down to me by my father. Some of this information was handed down from other people.

Daddy was born in Samaria "in Aiken County, South Carolina in 1904. (Samaria is a little settlement near New Holland and Wagener, South Carolina, outside of Aiken, South Carolina. Aiken is west of Augusta, Georgia toward Columbia, SC. His father was John Samuel Lybrand (called Sammie), who was born May 3, 1871 and died on November 28, 1924 of a rusty, barnyard nail scratch. The infected scratch turned into blood poisoning because he had diabetes. In 1924 there were no wonder drugs to fight such infections. Daddy was at Wofford College at the time. Daddy told me that he got a call from home, while at college, that his father was sick and to come home as soon as he could. He told me that he caught a train home and by the time he got there his father was already in a coma and died shortly thereafter.

His mother was Mamie Louise Clayton who was born July 7, 1878 and died on March 16, 1973. I know very little about my grandmother before she was married and where she came from. My daughter recently found out that the Claytons came over on the same ship from Germany that the Lybrand's came over on but two years earlier. I have looked and looked and have not been able to find out anything about her family. She told me that she lived quite a distance from where John Samuel lived and after the third or fourth date, she told John Samuel, "Let's just get married so that you can stop all this traveling back and forth that you are doing." Therefore that is what they did. They got married after dating only a few times.

Daddy was raised on a farm where his father grew just about everything they needed to eat. He mentioned crops like corn, wheat (for baking flour), sugar cane (for their sweetener), sweet potatoes, cotton (for a cash crop), figs, and garden vegetables. He also told me that they raised a few pigs (for meat), a cow for milk and butter, and chickens for eggs and meat. From what I could understand, they did not have to buy anything but a little salt and a few other items that they could not raise. Daddy told me that his father sold most of his excess produce in Augusta, Georgia, which is about an hour from his farm by car. I cannot imagine going that far by mule cart. He did mention that his Daddy bought a car later on.

One story that I vividly remember that dealt with Granddaddy's weight was when Granddaddy John Samuel was taking eggs to Augusta to sell, and on the way, three dozen were cracked, and he could not sell them. He took them to a restaurant and had them cook them. He sat down and ate all three dozen eggs to keep them from going to waste. Daddy told me that he weighed about 300 pounds, and you can see why from this story. One picture that I have included shows him about twice as large as the others in the photograph.

Another story that Daddy often told was that it was a real treat to get an ice cream cone in Augusta. On one occasion, his Daddy was eating some fig ice cream and really liked it. He felt a fig seed while eating the ice cream and was able to get it out of his mouth and took it home and raised a fig tree from the seed he found in the ice cream.

One interesting thing that Daddy told me was that in the second or third grade, he had a friend named Barnie. Daddy's given name was Harvey. Since Barnie spelled his name with an "i.e." Daddy thought his name was spelled wrong and changed it to Harvie, and no one tried to correct it. This misspelling was handed down to my brother, who was officially named Thomas Harvie Lybrand, and he handed down the misspelling to his son Thomas Harvie Lybrand, Jr. Therefore this misspelling had gone for three generations. One factor that may have had something to do with the changing of the spelling is that information that I have received about Daddy's father from some of his cousins refer to John Samuel as Sammie.

Daddy told me that his father weighed around 300 pounds and could lift a 500-pound bale of cotton. He also told me that his father was in such good shape that he could jump up and knocked his heels together three times before he landed. One sort of sad story that Daddy told me was that he almost talked his Daddy into buying him a bicycle.

His father also ran a general merchandise store in the area. One story that Daddy told me was that one day they went to the train station to pick up a few cases of canning jars. When they got there, there was a whole train car full of canning jars. Someone had made an error and sent him ten times the amount he ordered. Instead of sending them back, he carried them to his store and stacked the cases on top of each other about four cases high in a long line down the center of the store, and before the season was over, he had sold all of them.

When my father was 17 or 18 his father offered to build a store for him, give him a farm to work or he could go to college. He chose to go to college and went to Wofford in Spartanburg, South Carolina. One of the requirements for entry was a test on math and English. Since he had not had algebra, he purchased an algebra book and had the mailman teach him algebra the summer before he went to college to take his entrance exam. He related that during the exam, he felt the professor standing behind him watching him work out the problems he was working on. The professor grabbed bis paper and said, "Boy, you know what you are doing; you pass." Therefore he was able to start Wofford.

I recently came across Daddy's college grade cards, and the thing that got my attention was that he seemed to have been required to go an extra term before he went full time. I guess it was because the country school he attended lacked some of the requirements needed to get into Wofford. Another thing that impressed me was that every term, he took Bible and Military Science. He also took French and German. But his best grades were in math. He got a one or excellent in every math class he took. It appears that he entered college at age 18 in 1922 and graduated in 1926. On November 28, 1924, when my father was 19, and in college, his father died. He was commissioned as Second Lieutenant on March 12, 1926, at the age of 21.

My grandfather died while Daddy was in college and had credited most of the community. Only one person came to settle their debt with his family, and the family lost much of what my grandfather bad amassed during his lifetime. Therefore, Daddy had to borrow money to finish college. As this story has unfolded, you will see how this horrible experience affected how he raised me. He had me on my feet and running my own affairs very early in life. Because of this, I never had a whole summer off since age 13. He had me waiting on tables at the Ocean Villa at age 13.

He often mentioned the President of Wofford College, Dr. Henry W. Snyder, and referred to him as "Old Dr. Snyder." In college, in their foreign language classes, they were only allowed to speak the language they were taking. He often sang Silent Night, Holy Night in German, and would state how much prettier it was in German than in English. In his first math class, the professor shortly realized that his students could not add very well. Therefore, he stopped the class and gave his students rows of numbers and required them to run their finger down the line of numbers from top to bottom without stopping and then write the number down. He made them do this until everyone in the class could add any group of numbers, no matter how many numbers there were, without stopping. Until near his death, he could add any group of numbers much faster than you could do it on a calculator. He also could do amortization tables long hand. One of the courses he had in college was applied math or how you use the math you were taking. Not long after Mother died, I took him to the bank with a bunch of checks to be deposited. On the way home, he told me that they had shorted him a dime. The next time I saw him, he told me they had credited him his dime.

When he was in a good mood, he often laughed about waking up one morning and finding "Old Dr. Snyder's" cow in the bell tower and how much trouble the school officials had getting that cow back down to earth. No one "fessed up" to doing this, and they had no earthly idea how the students got that cow up in the bell tower.

On another occasion, they went to chapel, which was required, and found a Model T Ford on the stage. Since the car could not be driven through the door, the students had to take the car apart and reassemble it on the stage. Again, no one "fessed up" to this prank. I guess teenagers and young adults never change, as he would say.

Because of the extensive Military Science courses he took in college, he was commissioned as a Second Lieutenant in the infantry in The Army of the United States on March 12, 1926. I have a copy of his commission. He never served in the active military service, but he did go to summer camp or some type of boot camp training. He often talked about trying to hold a mule's head down and finally getting tired of the mule jerking his head up and down and tied the mule's head to a fence post, and the mule jerked the fence post out of the ground. Of course, he caught it from the sergeant in charge of his group.

He also often talked about being given a machine gun and tearing the target up without any real training. When he was asked where he learned to shoot that well, he told them it was just a gun, and he often hunted on his Daddy's farm. This is about all I know about his younger years except he worked very hard while living on his father's farm, and as a result, he could fix or build anything he put his mind to.

Since he graduated from college after the First World War and was around 40 years old when the Second World War started and because he was in the school business, he did not get called up for active duty. (As a sideline, later in his life, Governor Strom

Thurmond thought so much of him that he made him an honorary Colonel in the South Carolina Militia.)

I never heard him say what his major in college was, but it is evident from all the education courses he took that it was Education. He started in New Holland, South Carolina as a teacher and then became the principal of Pelion High School. I often heard how he gave his nephews (sons of his older sister, Thelma) a whipping in New Holland School for misbehaving when they were not much younger than he was at the time. I remember his nephews talking about what Uncle Harvie did to them in school and even giving his own kin a hard time. From Columbia on Hwy. 302, you come to Pelion first, then Wagener. From Wagener, you take a county road to New Holland and then to Aiken, SC.

After college, he could not get a job, so he spent about a year traveling all over the country selling magazine subscriptions. He related that he made enough to barely feed himself. During this year, he took a job as a driver of a station wagon that toured teachers all over the country. The trip he drove for was out west. He made enough to pay for his meals, and he stated that he got to see a lot of the country, which made the time go by quickly since he still could not find a permanent job.

One story I can remember about a trip he took out west with these teachers was that one teacher brought a large clay jug that was always in the way. On this tour, they stopped each night and camped out next to the station wagon they were traveling in. In the evening, the driver had to unload and set up the camp and then tear the camp down the following morning and get back on the road. One day, he saw some bears down by the river they had camped near for the scenery, and he decided to get rid of that big jug. While everyone was talking, he slipped several pieces of candy in that large jug and took it down where the bear would find it and quietly came back to camp. Of course, the bear shortly smelled the candy and started slapping the jug around, trying to get the candy out. Since the bear was making so much noise, everyone looked to see what was going on and saw the bear tearing up the large jug. No one "fessed up" to putting the jug down where the bear could find it. The drivers told the crowd that the bear must have stolen it from all the belongings on the ground, looking for something to eat. Thus, one worrisome thing was eliminated. Later, he came back from the summer tours, in 1927, he found a job teaching school in the New Holland Grammar School, which included the first through the seventh grade. The school was very close to where he was raised. One report I have received indicated that he taught math.

In my search for anything I could find out about Daddy's early life, I got a handwritten letter from an older gentleman named George Marion Lybrand who lived in West Columbia, SC. Here is the letter that was in his handwriting:


November 7, 2011


*Dear Sam,*

*Your letter was sent to my wife. I am giving you what I can remember. Remember your Grandmother Mamie that lived in New Holland with your father, Charlie (Jack) and Susie (Sue). Jack soon moved to Charleston. Sue had some typewriters in the home and taught typing. Probably funded under some program by F.D.R.*

*Your Father taught school at New Holland. He taught me in a math class in the fifth or sixth grade about 1931. Once he gave us a math exam and I was the only one to make 100.*

*He also taught penmanship called the Palmer Method. Instead of moving your fingers to write you kept your fingers still and moved your arm.*

*He ran for Superintendent of Education of Aiken County and was elected and moved to Aiken. I don't know how long he served. Later he went to work for a text book publishing company (The Laidlaw Brothers?) and moved to Edisto Island.*

*Also at times your cousin Rhett, Ray and Kenneth and Francis Hydrick stayed with your Grandmother and went to school at New Holland.*

21

With this letter it appears that Daddy started teaching at the New Holland Grammar School and then got the job as Principal of the Pelion High School. Daddy never really talked about teaching in New Holland. He only talked about Pelion High School. Therefore I did not know where he started teaching until I got this letter.

Since the Depression came along soon after he started to work and the only pay he got was promissory notes that he could take to the grocery store and get their value in food, he started seeking a job other than teaching. Shortly after he applied for and became principal of Pelion High School, the position of Superintendent of Education of Aiken County came open. Two older gentlemen in the community had occupied this position for quite some time, and many just assumed that they would continue in this elected position from then on.

About six months before the election, when he was struggling to make ends meet, he was talking to an older gentleman about the future in education. The older man told him that the Aiken County Superintendent of Education job was coming up for election and that if he did what he told him to do, he could beat these other two older gentlemen. He was 29 at the time. This was in 1932, right in the middle of the Depression. His older friend told him to go around to church outings, country stores, and civic groups and just tell stories and make them laugh until they got to know him. He told him to just mention in passing that he was running for Superintendent of Education and could do a good job since he was already in the school business and young enough to handle such a big job for them in hard times. Of course, he then asked for their votes.

He did just that and became a great after-dinner speaker and went on to win the election and thus got a real paying job. He served one four-year term and part of a second term. During his time, he gradually paid off the county school debts as tax money came in and even had a few new schools built. One day he was taking the maid home, and, as they passed schools he had built, he told the maid that he had built these schools. She popped up and told him he must be tired after building all those schools. I guess she assumed that he had actually built these schools by himself.

He was a busy man and must have gotten around a bit because he met and married my mother, Jennie Brown Owens, in 1932, the year he became Superintendent of Education. After they got married, they lived in Pelion for a while. But shortly after they got married, Daddy became aware of a nice vacant house in downtown Aiken that the bank-owned. He approached the bank and offered to start making payments on the house, with no down payment, if they would allow him to move in with his new wife. The bank agreed because the vacant house was a burden, and by doing this they would at least be getting a return on the house.

Mother grew up in Aiken. She was a beautiful lady, and in her later years, she was said to be the prettiest older lady anyone knew. She was very popular with the gentlemen and dated many of them. When she told her sisters she was getting married, they said, "Will you please tell us who you are going to marry?" Their first child, Tommy, came along in 1933 while they were living in the house Daddy bought from the bank.

After serving for four years and doing a good job for Aiken County, he ran again and was reelected. His claim to fame was that he won this second election and the famous Senator Strom Thurmond, who Daddy knew because he ran in the next county, ran for some other public office and lost. They were friends, and Daddy got a kick out of it. Rumors were that my Mother also dated Strom Thurmond. At least the three of them ran in the same social circle in those days during the Depression.

Not long after he began his second term as Superintendent of Education, a large family-owned book company out of Atlanta, Georgia, named Laidlaw School Book Company, came to South

Carolina looking for a salesman. They were offering $800.00 per month for a good salesman to represent them in the whole state. Daddy was about 33 years of age at the time.

The Laidlaw officials went to see the State Superintendent of education and asked if he could make any recommendations. He told them to go talk to Harvie Lybrand over in Aiken because he was young and was doing a great job for Aiken County. They did and offered him the job at $800.00 per month, which was a great salary at this time in history. His friends told him he was crazy to leave an elected job with a guaranteed salary with four more years for one that may or may not last. He took the job, resigned as Aiken County Superintendent and went on the road selling books.

I have included more about my Daddy in Chapter 3 which is about all of my ancestors and how he fit into my line.


These are the dates of importance in my Daddy's life until we moved to Edisto. *

| DATE | AGE | WHAT HE WAS DOING |
| --- | --- | --- |
| 1904 | 0 | He was born |
| 1922 | 18 | Entered Wofford |
| 1924 | 20 | His Father died |
| 1926 | 21 | Finished Wofford |
| 1926 | 21 | Took the year off and traveled USA |
| 1927 -1932 * | 22 - 29 | Taught at New Holland Grammar school and became principal of Pelion High School. |
| 1932 | 29 | Became Superintendent of |

| | | |
|---|---|---|
| | | Education, got married and bought a house in Aiken. |
| 1933 | 30 | Thomas Harvie Lybrand (Tommy) was born. |
| 1936 | 33 | Elected to 2nd term as Superintendent of Education of Aiken County, SC.Went to work for Laidlaw Book Co. |
| 1937 | 34 | *George Samuel Lybrand* (Sammie/me) was born. |
| 1939 (est.) | | He became District Governor of the Lions Club (In the Aiken area - not sure of the area he covered.) |
| 1941 | 38 | *David Ladson Lybrand* was born. |

*The dates and Daddy's age are not clear to me. These are estimates from what I have been told .The letter I received from the older gentleman, that I have included, stated that it was during 1931 when Daddy taught in New Holland. I am not sure of these dates. All I can say is that Daddy started teaching in New Holland and then went to Pelion which is about 15 to 20 miles away but considered the same general community.

I came along in 1937 and the next major event in Daddy's life was buying a house on Edisto in 1942. He continued traveling and selling books. Mother and us boys spent the summers from 1942 to 1947 on the beach during the week and Daddy came on the weekends. We moved full time to Edisto Beach in the fall of 1947. Daddy was 38 when we began to spend the summers on Edisto Beach.

The following is what I can remember that Daddy told me about his early years selling books. He was making sales in the large schools in Columbia, Greenville, Spartanburg, and Florence, but when he went to the smaller schools, the principals were hard to deal with, so he started avoiding them. He soon noticed that his competition was doing the same. Therefore, he decided to call on the bigger schools one week of the month and then spend the next three weeks calling on the smaller schools because there were more of them. He would call on the principals of these small schools and take them to lunch or offer to play golf with them and just try to make friends with them and put up with their idiosyncrasies. As a result, he made friends out of all these principals of small schools that as a group bought more books than all the big schools put together. In a couple of years, he tripled the volume of books he sold. These principals made up the core of those that began to come to the Ocean Villa in later years.

As time went on after Daddy had bought the Edisto Beach house where we spent the summers, Daddy was always building things in our Aiken backyard to take to Edisto to improve the old beach house. It seems that every time we headed out for the beach, there was a trailer behind our car. The trip was a three-hour trip, and I remember Barnwell being the first leg of the trip. Then came Walterboro. When we got to Walterboro, I knew we were about there.

A couple of years before we started going to Edisto, the "Bomb Plant," as most called it, came to town. It seemed that people from all over the nation came to the Savannah River Plant to work. I remember fields upon fields were covered with travel trailers where people lived while working at the "Bomb Plant." All I heard, and it meant little to me, was that this operation was to provide material for the Atomic Bomb. I am still not sure what they actually do to this date. Several of Mother's family got involved in this vast operation.

It seems that things at home built up as Tommy kept causing trouble, and Mother's mother was living with us. All I remember about my Grandmother was that I had nothing to do with her and that she was hard to get along with. I often said she was as mean as a snake. George and Ed, Mother's brothers, were constantly coming over, getting into the mix while Daddy was off trying to make a living. Plus, Mother had two small children. It all seemed to come to a head when Mother suddenly started crying and kept on crying until she had to be taken to what I was told was a sanatorium for electric shock treatments.

I guess that Daddy being gone most of the week, Tommy causing trouble, George and Ed coming over, David coming along in 1941, a war going on, her mother living with us and me being sickly just got the best of her. Daddy decided he could travel just as well from Edisto as he could from Aiken and moved us to the beach, as I have already said, for the summers from 1942 to 1947.

One of Daddy's favorite stories that he told me over and over again about trips he took after he retired was about a group tour he took down into Mexico. It seems that the bus group he was traveling with stopped at a roadside stand to just look around and stretch their legs. While he was there, he saw a man give five dollars to the owner of the roadside stand. The owner then opened a bottle of beer and gave it to his favorite mule. The mule took the bottle between his front teeth and turned up his head and chugalugged it down without stopping. Daddy saw the pyramids of Egypt and the wall of China but this was his favorite story of things that impressed him the most while he traveled around the world. He just could not get over seeing that mule drink that bottle of beer with gusto.

The rest of Daddy's story is covered in the first part of this book and in the section on my ancestors. The following is how • I viewed Aiken before we moved to Edisto. While writing this book it surprised me what I remembered. Again, all of these events are not in a chronological order. They are just my recollections. This section also covers many things about my mother that I have not already covered.

On the next page are a few more early pictures of Daddy.

Early picture of Sue, Daddy,
Granny & Jack in
New Holland, SC

Daddy with Tommy In
Aiken, SC

Picture taken about 1943 of Daddy,
Mother, Mother's mother Tommy,
Me and David

Daddy in his early
years

# George Samuel (Sam) Lybrand April 3, 1937 - To Present (2012)

Let me start from the beginning again. I was born on April 3, 1937, in the Aiken County Hospital. Aiken is across the Savannah River from August, Georgia. Aiken is a beautiful small town with the reputation of being one of the main centers for horse racing in South Carolina. Therefore, it attracted many wealthy people that were into horse racing and into polo, known as the game of kings. Early on in Aiken's development, many northerners came to Aiken for the racing season and stayed in several grand hotels and inns.

My father traveled to South Carolina selling school books, and my mother was a stay-at-home mom, which was the norm in the 1930s. Our family did not mix with the wealthy people in Aiken but had a comfortable lifestyle on my father's salary. Mother had many brothers and sisters and much of our social life revolved around her family. My father's family came from the New Holland, SC, area about 12 miles from Aiken on the way to Columbia, SC. We also spent quite a bit of time visiting my father's mother in New Holland before we moved to Edisto.

I was the second of three children born into our family. According to my Mother, I was stillborn, and the doctor could not get me to start breathing the normal way. In desperation, the doctor put his mouth to my very tiny mouth and lightly breathed into my lungs to inflate them. Of course, this worked, or I would not be writing this book for my children and grandchildren.

My earliest recollection of our family home in Aiken, SC, at 1441 Park Avenue was that it was a large brick house, as a child sees it. It had a front porch with square columns with brick stairs that went directly down to the sidewalk in front of our house. On the left side of the house facing the street was a one-car carport where Daddy parked his car. I can still remember the old rounded fender car with two doors.

One of my earliest memories is of the mailman coming up on our front porch and putting the mail in a little metal box hanging near the front door. I guess I remembered this because, from the inside of the house, you could hear him shut the metal box's top door after he had put the mail in it. I guess he shut it hard so the people on the inside could hear that he had delivered the mail. I later saw him walking down the street every morning with his large sack of mail.

Of course, every kid remembers his brother and sisters. I was one of three boys; Tommy was the oldest and was approximately four years older than me. Tommy's b1rthday was April 5, 1933. I was the second child and was called Sammie. My birthday is on April 3, 1937. David was the youngest, and he was born approximately four years after me. David's birthday is June 23, 1941. As a result of these age differences, we three boys had little to do with each other until we got older. A four-year-old and a baby do not play with each other. I especially remember that Tommy had little to do with me because I was so much younger than he was. Plus, I was sickly most of the time, as I remember. I have little recollection of what Tommy did and who he played with him other than he played football in the back yard with Billy Jackson, our next-door neighbor, and some other boys from down the street. I don't remember the other boys' names. I only sat by and watched them because I was too little to play with the big boys. My first recollection of Tommy was seeing him walking away from the house after an argument with Daddy and trying to follow him. He told me to go back home. The thing that stands out about Tommy was that he was always causing trouble, which followed him throughout his life until his untimely death on January 18, 1972, at the age of 38. From him, I learned that if you were going to live a long and contented life, you had to conform and join the community in which you lived. If you are going to live a normal life, there are some things you do and something you don't do. If you are going to make anything of yourself, there are things that are expected of you. The sooner you learn these things, the better you will be and the happier and more contented you will be.

For some strange reason, I remember that mother had several large strainers that she pushed beans and other vegetables through with a large wooden stick of a sort that she fed to David. I guess this was before you went to the store and bought all kinds of baby food for your children. At least this is what we did for our own children. As I am writing this, it surprises what I remember and what I don't remember. Keep in mind that I was 75 years old when I started this.

Our house had a front room with a fireplace we called the living room (I never heard about a den until after I was married), a dining room and a kitchen with a small porch on the back of the house. There was another porch off the back bedroom. The other side of the house had three bedrooms and one bath. My parents' room was upfront, then came the bath. Next were two other bedrooms. All three of us boys used the back bedroom.

The bathroom stands out because I remember David locking himself in it and cutting on the water. Daddy had to call the fire department to come in the back yard and use a long ladder to get into a small bathroom window over the tub so they could open the bathroom door from the inside. I can remember it all being a mess. Also, outside of this bathroom window was the prettiest flower I ever remember seeing as a child. Mother called it a coral vine. It has small pink or red flowers that form a big bunch of red flowers. The vine climbed a wire up the house from the backyard to where it came into the house and then out the wire a good ways. You could see the flowering vine from the backyard and from the bathroom window. I just remember how beautiful it looked. I guess this was the first flower I ever took much notice of. It is strange what kind of things stick out in a child's memory. For some reason, the memory of this pretty vine keeps coming up when I think of our house in Aiken.

A hall was between the living area and the bedrooms. Off this hall was a staircase that led downstairs to a furnace room or basement. A large truck would come every so often and dump coal down a chute to a coal bin in the furnace room. This bin had boards on the front that were taken off, one by one as the coal was used up. I remember this room as being damp and hot. It was open to the backyard, so our cats came and went as they pleased. I remember the cats having kittens down there. We seemed to always have cats around the house. The female cats would have many kittens, and sometimes the tomcats came around and killed all the male kittens. I later learned that they did this to reduce their competition later on. I guess the downstairs area is what you would now call a basement. The basement or furnace room only took up one half of the area below the house.

I remember Daddy talking about turning the basement into an apartment to rent for more income. I heard him tell someone that he went to the lumber yard and told the owner that he wanted to turn his basement into an apartment. He needed so many board feet of lumber and asked the lumber yard owner to give it to him on time. The owner was not selling much lumber at the time and readily agreed. This must have happened in the early 1940s because I remember it being built. Daddy did most of the work himself. I guess he learned how to do all this from working on the farm. It used to amaze me how much he knew about so many things. I remember Daddy telling someone that before he had it finished, a couple heard about it and asked to rent it. It seemed that it stayed rented.

I remember one renter as being a jockey who raced horses at the local racetrack. He stood out because he seemed to be not much bigger than us kids. He also stood out because he was friendly and played with us from time to time. He was just one of the kids.

Because of this jockey, I can remember being taken to the racetrack to watch the horse races. I seem to enjoy watching the races between small horse-drawn buggies. I don't remember what they called these tiny little buggies behind these fast-moving horses. But I do remember the horses walking real fast and not running like the regular horses did. It seemed that every time we went to the racetracks, everyone was having a great time like you would have at a county fair. Everyone seemed to be excited and talking about this horse or that horse. I could never remember the names of any horses or really what was going on. I just remember everyone having a good time and how excited I was to see all this activity going on all at once.

One thing that stands out in my mind is standing behind a white wooden fence and watching all the horses come thundering past me as they raced by. I was not tall enough to watch them over the top of the fence. I watched the horses through the long fence rails that made up the fence. All these horses running full speed ahead was something almost unbelievable in my eyes as a young boy. I mostly saw only the legs and all the dirt they were kicking up as they went by. As they raced by, it seemed that I was looking directly into a storm or commotion of unimaginable chaos.

When I think about the racetrack, I remember riding by very large houses with very large magnolia trees in the front yard. The yards were always very green and neat. The houses were hard to see for all the large trees in the front yard. Strangely, I never saw any of these people and often wondered if they were real. I was told that rich people owned these houses and that they came down from the north during the winter for the racing season.

Mother's older brothers, Uncle George and Uncle Ed, used to dig up these large trees and move them to these rich people's yards so they could have a ready-made impressive front yard. It was almost unbelievable how my uncles dug these large trees up using all kinds of ropes and pulleys and then loaded them onto a truck and moved them to these rich people's yards.

**Rabbit Trail:** Let me stop right here and tell you that I am writing this at age 75, but my memories about Aiken stopped when we left Aiken. It seems a little strange that I am telling this as if I were a young child. What I thought was a large back yard then turned out to be rather small when I went back many years later. I guess that if you are four feet tall and something is six feet high, six feet seemed high. But when you got six feet tall and see a six feet high object, it does not seem so high. Therefore all of my recollections of Aiken come from the perspective of a small kid. Some of my recollections have come from stories my father told me that I had the good sense to write down over the years. The book is an attempt to get all that I know about Aiken and Edisto in one place. The details of what I remember seemed a little strange until I was tested in the service and found that I had a very high mechanical aptitude and very high creative ability. I just have always observed how things work and seem to remember them forever. My English ability is limited; therefore, I speak very plainly, which seems to be very understandable. All this has seemed to have come together as I tried to put down on paper what I know and remember about my past for my children and grandchildren. **Back to our yard**

On the left facing the street, our yard was level. On the right side and in the back of the house, it was dug out to make two levels. A large brick wall ran from the back of the house on the left, almost to the back to the lot. A road went around the back of this wall to allow a car to get into the lower level and for the people that were renting the apartment to get to their apartment. A set of brick steps on the left allowed us to go from the street level to the lower back yard. The other side of the yard was down about four to five steps, and another set of brick steps was next to the front sidewalk and separated the upper level from the lower level. I remember that Mother had a flower bed behind this front wall on both sides of the steps that went from the sidewalk down to the back yard. I could sit on these steps and see the coral vine blooming on the wire that came into the house. I could also sit on these steps and see the door of the apartment that Daddy built that opened to the lower level yard. I remember playing with a small dog on these steps that belonged to one of the people who rented this apartment.

It seemed that we had the only open back yard, and a bunch of kids would come over to play football with Tommy, as I have already mentioned. Once I remember them giving the ball to me, and I turned around and ran the other way because a bunch of big boys were coming at me. I guess I was small and not much of an athlete while we lived in Aiken.

In the back yard were two large weeping willow trees planted in the back of the lot. We used to break off the hanging branches and make whips out of them. For some reason, Mother and Daddy did not mind us breaking up these willow trees. There was also a large outside "fireplace/barbeque pit" that was made out of rocks that Daddy brought home from all over the state. I remember these rocks being very pretty and of different colors. I can also remember there was a large black washpot back there that Daddy and Tommy cooked boiled peanuts in to sell somewhere downtown. I can also remember all of mother's family coming and having large family reunions in our backyard. From my perspective, it seemed that there were a thousand people at these family reunions.

In the back of our house was a railroad cut. A cut is a ditch cut into the ground to make the track as level as possible for the train track. On our side of the railroad cut, it was about four feet deep. On the other side of the cut, it was well over a man's head. Larger children had cut footholds into the red clay bank so they could more easily climb out of the cut. Daddy had a large vegetable garden between our property's fence and the railroad cut. I guess they let us use the land because Daddy kept it clean, and the railroad people did not have to keep it up. This garden was called a Victory Garden because during the Second World War, it was expected of everyone to grow as much food as possible so that the nation's energy could go to the war effort.

It was like having your own large train track set up in your backyard. I loved watching these big steam engines puffing up the hill toward the station below our house. It was a pure delight to see these trains come by our house. I was so unhappy when the strange-looking square boxes that made very little noise replaced the large steam engines. One steam engine could pull many rail cars, but it took two or three of the strange-looking boxes to pull the same amount of rail cars. You could hear the old steam engines coming up the track from a long way off, and you had plenty of time to go to the fence and wave to the man running the steam engine. In fact, everything seemed to shake as these large old engines went by. Also, long before the old steam engines got to our house, you could see the smoke coming from the engines as they burned coal. I can still remember seeing a man shoveling coal into the fire that heated the water than ran the engine. You could see the red glow from the fire as the engines went by. I guess I should not tell this, but we played in the railroad cut and would put nails and pennies on the tracks and watch the wheels of the train mash them flat. Of course, we would get out of the cut before the train came because we could see it coming way down the track. We could also tell it was coming a long way off by putting our ears to the track.

We lived on a corner. I don't remember the name of the street that came off of Park Avenue. There was a bridge on this street that went over the railroad track. When the steam engines came under the wooden bridge beside our house, the smoke would come up through the wooden boards in the bridge. I was always excited to see all the smoke, almost hiding the bridge as a train went under. From time to time, some of the local boys would try to stand on the edge of the bridge and throw rocks down the smokestack of the train as it went under the bridge. But the train put out so much smoke that the boys would have to give up because the smoke would overwhelm them. Also, under the bridge was a sort of cave under where the road stopped, and the bridge road began. This was a great hideout. I guess it was not a very safe place because there was only a small ledge between where the bridge's wooden structure started and where the dirt dropped off down to the cut. In thinking about this, I began to think that we all need to take some chances in life if we are to get anywhere. I guess those that learn to be careful coming up, but not too careful as not to experience any adventures, are the ones that seem to get ahead later in life. As the old saying says, "No risk, no gain."

I spent many hours building all kinds of things with erector sets, tinker toys, and Lincoln logs. As stated before, I still like to build things. I think I am the most satisfied when I am creating this or that. Now I am at the stage in life where my grandchildren often give me orders for what they want me to build for them. My favorite things to build are secret boxes. I build fancy little wooden boxes with bright hinges and locks. They can put then on their dressers to keep their special things in. I try to make everyone different and out of different types of wood. I give one key to the child and one key to the mother in case the child loses his key.

One day an unscheduled troop train came by and put out a flare. At the time, we did not know that it put out the flare to warn other trains that it was ahead of them and to slow down. Well, this particular flare caught the grass on the track on fire and was about to burn up our garden. So some of the neighborhood boys put the fire out and removed the red flare. Shortly thereafter, the regularly scheduled train came along, and all of a sudden, we heard all this squealing and noise as the second train almost ran into the troop train. We then knew why the first train had put down the flare. Nothing ever came of it, so we did not get in trouble. But we all loved these big old steam engines and considered it very nice to live next to the railroad tracks. I knew I was not supposed to go down into the railroad cuts, but I did it anyhow. I guess children just are drawn to places they are told to stay away from.

Long green looking troop trains often came by taking boys to war, and all sorts of special looking trains came by our house. You could see all the soldiers dressed in their uniforms. Some were hanging their arms out the windows and just taking life as it was and not seeming to be disturbed by where they were going. With no TV or much to entertain us, these large steam engines filled a void and made life more interesting. Because of my years on Edisto and all its adventure, I feel sorry for young people that seemed to be bored when there is so much to learn about all around them. I surely was interested in everything that went on around me and took it all in. By being interested in what was going on around me growing up, I can now build just about anything I can measure or see a picture of because I was interested enough to watch how things were built and how many things worked. I found myself taking apart many of my toys to see how they worked.

The road that went past our house and over the bridge went another block and then came to a crossroad. If you turned right, you could see our grammar school two blocks away. I can remember walking to the first grade from my home. I remember a little girl that lived on one of the two blocks that lead from the road past our house to my school as being named Cammie. I remember it because it rhymed with my name. I was called Sammie until I started going to college. Some people that knew me as a child still call me Sammie. I was named after my two grandfathers named John Samuel Lybrand and George Edmund Owens. My grandfather, John Samuel Lybrand, was also called Sammie. Therefore I was called Sammie. Some say I have his personality - always laughing and cutting up.

I started kindergarten at this very large two-story red brick school not far behind the courthouse and fronting on Whiskey Road. I remember the name of the road name because Uncle George and Ed owned a farm on Whiskey Road. The schoolhouse was just a plain building with no frills. It did have a large playground in the back with little or no playground equipment. All I remember about this school was that when I first started out, they made us take a nap on mats laid out on the floor. I don't remember actually sleeping on these mats - just lying there waiting for the time to be up. The start of the Second World War does stick in my mind with the bombing of Pearl Harbor. I am sure I had no idea where Pearl Harbor was. I just knew that it was someplace important because most of the people around me were excited and wondering what would happen next. I remember how sad people were when President Roosevelt died. Another thing that stands out in the fourth grade was that the teacher would hold up multiplication tables cards until all of us knew them by heart. It was drill and drill until we all got it. In my mind, this school building was large and impressive to me as a young kid. Other than these memories, I have no more memories of going to grammar school in Aiken. I guess it must have been a good experience and non-eventful, or I would have remembered more. One event did stand out. One day a boy I knew had his dog follow him to school, and while we were out on the playground, the dog lifted his leg and took a leak on another boy's leg. What strange things we seem to remember!

Our house was on a divided street. On one side of the street were houses. In the middle of the street was a large park, a city block long with lots of trees that all the kids in the neighborhood played in. I can remember the first time I was old enough and strong enough to start climbing the trees. I can remember a large bush that had what we called sugar tits on it. Of course, they must not have been poisonous because we all ate them. They were a little bitter, but we ate them anyhow.

One thing that stands out in my mind was that there was this nice ragged old tramp that used to cross our park from time to time. When we saw him, we would run up to him, and he would give each of us a piece of candy. I don't know anything else about this man other than he seemed to enjoy getting so much attention from so many children. As far as I know, he may have been an angel checking up on us and spreading joy among God's children during a hard time for all. There seemed to be a lot of trouble going on around us, but the kids in the neighborhood took it all in stride and made the best of it.

On the other side of the street was a shoe store that sold shoes and repaired old shoes. There was a grocery store and meat shop where you could get fresh cut meat. There was also a barbershop where I often got a haircut. For a long time, Mother kept my hair long in locks until Daddy put his foot down and made her take me across the street and get a little boy's haircut. I remember it was a big deal getting my hair cut for the first time. I know there were other stores, but I cannot remember what they were. But I do remember that Mother did not have to go anywhere else to buy whatever we needed to eat. Daddy would leave on Monday and come back Thursday or Friday. He would leave Mother with a ten-dollar bill that seemed to last all week. If it did not, I don't remember us having to do without until Daddy returned. Can you even imagine that in the early 1940s, it only took ten dollars to feed a family of five for a week?

When I was around six years old, I remember having trouble with a tonsil operation and having to go back to the hospital because of bleeding. The bright lights in the operating room stand out. I still often dream about hanging my head off the table with blood just gushing out of my mouth into a bowl held by a nurse. I vividly remember this actually happening, and I guess that the reason I keep dreaming about it because it must have been serious. I guess I survived because I am still here writing about it 70 years later.

I can also remember my Mother nursing David and mashing out some milk into a spoon for me to taste. I remember it being not very tasty and not asking about it again.

It seems that I was sickly because of having whooping cough at an early age and not gaining much weight. Shortly after getting over the whooping cough, I developed severe sinus problems. It seems that I was 37 pounds for quite some time, and Mother and Daddy were constantly trying to get me to eat. I still remember them constantly weighing me and the constant effort to try to get me to eat and gain weight. I don't think I will ever forget the number 37 because I heard it so much. I must have stayed at that weight for a long time. Because of my sinus problems coming up, Mother had to take me to Augusta, Georgia, to have my nose pumped out. I can remember stuff just coming and coming out of my nose. At home, Mother would put warm salty water up my nose and then suck out the stuff in my nose with something that looked like a large rubber eyedropper. I don't remember breathing through my nose until I was six years old. I still, to this date, breathe through my mouth most of the time at night.

I can remember when I first discovered that Santa Claus was not real. It seems that I was rummaging through one of our closets, which I liked to do, and seeing a windup airplane that just so happened to be under the Christmas tree on Christmas morning. It surely burst my bubble because I enjoyed the fact that there was a real Santa Claus. I can still remember lying in bed on Christmas Eve, thinking I saw Santa Claus flying through the air and wondering when he would get to our house. To me, it seemed real, and I still remember joyfully looking up into the blue, dark sky on Christmas Eve, thinking I saw Santa Claus.

As previously mentioned, from my earliest years, I can remember Tommy giving my parents a hard time and always getting into trouble. Of course, I got my share of spanking for not doing what I was told to do. Until the day my father died, I would have done anything he asked me to do because I respected him and knew that his word was the law. If I did not obey I knew the penalty was swift and certain. So overall, I obeyed as best as a young child can obey. But there was never any bate or disrespect for my father. When he got after me, I knew why he was getting after me and knew what was coming. To this day, I take orders well, and it has served me well. I got along well at The Citadel and in the service because I already knew how to follow orders and did not question my commanders' orders. We have lost a lot in America by not requiring our fathers to take charge of their families and to teach their children how to obey orders before they are put in a position to lead. You cannot lead if you first don't know how to take orders. When you take the leadership of the fathers away from the family or do not have an authoritarian in charge of a family, then the family falls apart. You get a bunch of children that grow up aimless with little or no direction, and thus the community and nation have lost. As I grow older, I realize that a child's first image of God is how his father and mother treat him. America has lost a great deal when it became almost a curse to mention God in polite conversations. How God would have us live is the most important thing all of us need to know.

It seems that all the boys slept in the same room, and when we went to bed, we would always get into a fight or cause some kind of unnecessary noise. One night one of us called out to Daddy and said, "Daddy, when you come to spank us, bring me a drink of water?" We seem to come to expect a spanking every night so that we would settle down and go to sleep.

My mother was a kind-hearted woman. Tramps would often come directly across our park to our back door and ask Mother for a sandwich. She would always feed them. There was a well-worn path across the park where tramps would come directly to our house. I guess the word got around among the tramps that this kind lady would feed you. I never heard her turn anyone these hard-up people down. She fed everyone that came to her door. This was in the late 1930s and early 1940s when things were still tough. It seemed in those days people really looked after each other and shared what little they had with the others around them. I do not remember any murder and theft. It seemed that people were not afraid to ask when they needed help. These same tramps that mother fed also rode the slow-moving freight trains. You could see several of them sitting in the doors of open boxcars with their legs hanging down as the trains went past our house. But thankfully, we always had enough to eat. Daddy always worked and seemed to have a good job even though he did travel most of the time.

One of my fondest memories was going to my grandmother's house (Daddy's mother). She lived in New Holland, South Carolina, about 12 miles from Aiken, and having Frances serve me hot biscuits that I dipped into hot honey and fresh cream. Frances called it sopping. The biscuits and honey just melted in my mouth. Frances treated me like a doll and played with me all the time. She was a beautiful young girl, about 16 to 18 years old at the time. Frances was Daddy's oldest sister's child. Daddy's sister, Thelma, died in childbirth having her fifth child when Frances was about one and a half years old. Daddy's mother took Frances in and raised her as if she was her own child. Therefore, when we went to Granny's house, Frances was always there. Daddy's sister Sue also lived with Granny for a while when we visited.

Granny lived on a small farm in New Holland, and it seems that she, Sue, and Frances ran it by themselves. As I have already noted, Granddaddy died about 13 years before I was born.

On the back and to the left of the old unpainted house, Granny lived in was a wrap-around porch with a hand pitcher pump where Granny got water. I can remember Daddy saying that he did not feel clean until his face was washed with a cold washrag. Out back was a barnyard with farm animals. Also out back was a two-hole privy where everyone went to the bathroom. At night if you had to go to the bathroom, you used a slop jar or a large white bucket with a rounded top edge so you could sit on it. It also had a lid to keep down the odor. Every morning these slop jars had to be emptied. But that was the way it was in most places in the country, and no one seemed to make much fuss about it.

One memory that sticks out in my mind was walking past Granny's bedroom and seeing Granny through a crack in the door sitting on the slop jar with her knees sticking up almost to her chin. Every time I think about this scene etched in my memory I get a good laugh. Out of respect for her, I never told Granny I saw her sitting on the slop jar.

Granny also had chickens. She would give me a few eggs that I could walk down to a store nearby and trade the eggs for candy. That always seemed like a treat.

I vividly remember Granny sweeping her backyard clean of any grass or trash so she could see any snakes that might be hiding in the yard. The broom she used was made of tree branches that were stripped of any leaves and tied together at the top with some strong string. I can still see her now bending over and sweeping the yard clean

The old house had some electric power. Lights bulbs were hung down from the ceiling on a single cord with a pull chain. I can remember the first time I was able to cut a ceiling light on from a switch on the wall in our house in Aiken. The house had the old gas light lamps still on the wall. I was told that they used to put water in a tank and then put carbide crystals in the water. It produced a gas that was carried to these lamp stands on the wall by copper pipes. There was a valve on each lamp that you had to cut on and light to make the carbide lamps give off light. Like gas lamps you had to light these lamps with a match when you wanted to light a room. I don't know why I remember so much about such things at so early an age. I guess it is because I have always been interested in how things work and would take mechanical toys apart to see how they worked. (Later in life I found out that I am mechanically minded and thought in things instead of words and numbers. Therefore, I have always been interested in how things work, even from an early age.)

Along these lines the old house had lighting rods on the end of each gable. These were fancy decorated rods that stuck up in the air about two to three feet with a large braided cable going down to a rod deep in the ground. I saw many houses in the area with these lighting rods on them but I never heard of anyone that was hit by lighting and these rods saving them. My estimate was that a very good salesman sold all these people on the benefit of putting lighting rods on their houses to protect them from a lightning strike.

I can remember Granny going out to the woodpile and cutting up very small pieces of wood to fire up her wood burning stove. Someone had cut large round slabs out of large pine trees and brought them to her. Granny would take a hatchet and chop small straight pieces very easily from one of the round slabs to keep her wood stove hot. These stove pieces were about one inch by two inches by six inches long or how thick the slab was. The stove was a large cast iron stove with four round removable plates at the top that you could put a frying pan on to cook. You removed these round plates with an iron handle of some type. The handles stayed cool enough to remove these hot plates. It also had a large oven door with an oven to bake pies and cakes. It seems like the kitchen was always hot because of this wood stove. Granny would keep putting these small pieces of wood in the stove to keep the fire burning in the stove so she could keep cooking.

One of the things that tickled me the most was seeing Granny get rid of the flies in her house. All the rooms in the house opened to the wrap around porch and were connected on the inside. She would open the back screened door and go through the house with a large white sheet, flapping it back and forth and holding onto two corners of the sheet so it would cover a large area. She would open the door leading to the next room and run all the flies to the next room. Then she would quickly close the door behind her and open the next door and start flapping the sheet until she got all the flies out of that room. He would continue this until she came to the kitchen and then run all the flies out the open back door. It would be days before any flies were found in the house. I only saw her do this once.

Another thing that fascinated me about Granny's place was the smokehouse and how she stored sweet potatoes. Most of the meat we ate came from the smokehouse. I am not sure how she got the meat in the smokehouse but it was always full of smoked meat. Of course, it always smelled like smoke even a good distance away from it. Granny stored her extra sweet potatoes in hill as she called them. These hills had a two-foot diameter hole dug into the ground that was lined with pine straw. The hills were banked up around the top to keep the surface water from going into them and they were covered with a piece of old tin to keep the rain water from getting in the top. The sweet potatoes were placed in this hole and covered with dirt. When you wanted a sweet potato you just went to the hill and dug out the amount of potatoes you wanted. It seemed that Granny had it all figured out and could live with very little help from anyone. Granny stayed busy all the time working hard but she made it all work and everyone seemed well fed. I loved going to see and staying with my Grandmother, Frances and Sue. Of course, you can see that I was partial to Frances.

One thing that got my attention was seeing large fields near where Granny lived planted with asparagus. Many times, we would stop by these fields and see men behind two large horses plowing the fields. Sometimes we'd see two or more pairs of horses plowing the same large field. Since then I have been told that asparagus was a popular and very profitable crop in this area at that time and many acres were planted in asparagus. When writing this I asked myself why a child would remember asparagus. I am sure I did not know what an asparagus was or even what it looked like. I think the thing that impressed me was seeing the large horses yoked together and a man walking behind them. There was not only one but several working these large fields. As I have related before it has been interesting to me what I remember and what I don't remember.

On the way to Granny's house, not far from our house, there was a large pond at the bottom of a hill where we often went to swim and sit around with other people the family knew. I remember there were always many people around this pond. It seemed that it also had a restaurant or a place to eat. I remember how clear the water was. Happy memories come to mind when I think about this old pond. It seems that some of the happiest times I had growing up were going to and staying with Granny because there were so many interesting things to explore. On the way to Granny's house there were large houses sitting right in the middle of farm land with large trees growing on both sides of the roads leading to these impressive houses.

Later Granny came to live with us and I remember she made me peach and blackberry cobblers that just melted in my mouth. To this day I like cobblers because they remind me of happy times. I don't remember how long Granny lived with us but I do remember that she went to live with Aunt Sue who had moved to Charleston, South Carolina to work at the Navy Yard. Frances also went down to live with Sue when Granny went. As a young child we often went to Charleston to visit Granny, Sue and Frances. I am not sure when they moved to Charleston but Daddy's brother Uncle Jack lived in Charleston also. We would go see Uncle Jack when we went to see Granny. These visits are sketchy at best. I am not sure how old I was when we started going to visit Granny in Charleston. I do remember that Sue lived. close to a very busy highway and a fire station in what they called North Charleston. It seems that the fire station was only a few buildings away from where Sue lived.

When we moved to Edisto, I can remember going to see Granny and Sue on several Christmas afternoons and seeing many black children riding their new bicycles and roller skating all over the road near where Sue lived because there was very little traffic on Christmas day. We all noticed that they seemed to be having the time of their lives.

One thing that sticks out in my mind about Granny is that once I told Daddy how much I loved Granny and how nice she was. He got a little mad looking and said I did not know the half of it. He said his mother was a holy terror. It seemed that Granny was always telling my mother what to do and getting after her when she did not do what Granny told her to do. He used an example as follows; Mother asked Granny how to make fig preserves and she told her. Mother did exactly what Granny told her and the figs cooked up to little knobs. She told Granny what happened and Granny told her that any fool would know you had to add water as you heated the figs because some of the water would boil away as it cooked. Of course, when Granny called Mother a fool, she got mad and complained to Daddy about how his mother treated her. I guess children only see only one side of some stories.

I remember that we took at least one vacation to the Smoky Mountains. I remember staying in a cabin next to a pond we could swim in. At meal time we would walk across the dam of the pond to a dining room that seemed open with only a roof covering it. We took many side trips around the mountains. The thing that stands out in my memory is that Daddy bought me a small pocket knife and I lost it soon after we started back to our cabin. Daddy and Mother took the car apart trying to find that knife and never found it. This seemed to have spoiled the whole trip for me. To this day and for most of my adult life I have carried one or more pocket knives in my pocket all the time. In fact, I feel undressed if I don't have a pocket knife in my pocket.

Mother's mother also came to live with us during my early years after Granny had left. All I remember about her was that she was mean and had very little to do with me. Because of this and maybe some other things, I can remember waking up during the night hearing my Mother crying and screaming until Daddy took her off to have electric shock treatment. They seemed awful at the time and I thought they might kill my mother. When she came home, she was confused about who was who. I can remember riding in the back of the car listening to Daddy tell her who lived where and telling her all about our town.

We lived about four blocks from town. As I got a little older Mother would give me a dime and I would walk downtown with several of the other kids on the block on Saturday mornings and go to see movies that continued on and on with the same story week after week. Just before the hero would get killed it would stop and start over the next week. You had to come back the next week to see how our hero got out of trouble. Of course, each movie started with a cartoon. It just was not a movie without a cartoon. The heroes at this time were Roy Rogers, the Lone Range rand his sidekick Tonto and other cowboys I have forgotten. But I am sure about Roy Rogers and the Lone Ranger. Even in college movies started with a cartoon. "The Road Runner and the Coyote" was our all-time favorite. Even today I feel that there is something missing when a movie does not start with a cartoon.

One Friday I remember I had the choice of going to see "Bambi" or going to spend the night with my cousin Marion Eubanks. Marion was my age and lived on a dairy farm out in the country not far from Aiken. Marion was Mother's oldest sister's fourth child and we played together every chance we had. I loved to go there and see all the cows and such. But this particular time I was tom between going to see "Bambi" or going to spend the night with Marion. Well, I decided to go spend the night with Marion. During the night I got homesick and Daddy had to come get me early the next morning. It seemed that it was still dark when he came to get me. I guess I was causing a lot of trouble and my aunt wanted me out of her house and back at my house. I remember homesickness as being very bad and making you feel awful. So I did not get to visit Marion as planned and I also missed seeing "Bambi." I still remember this loss to this day. Being homesick seemed awful and like I would not live if I did not get back home. I did not get to see the movie "Bambi" until I took my own children to see it later in life.

Later when visiting Marion, I saw calves being born and how a dairy farm worked. I was always amazed that cows got milked in a certain order. The top cow got milked first. Then each cow was called by name and she came in to be milked. If the pecking order got out of line a fight would break out among the cows. How they knew all the names of these cows and who was top cow etc. was beyond my thinking. After often visiting this farm no one had to explain the birds and bees to me.

One of the things I liked to do was walk downtown with Mother and go into the department store. When we got in the store, I would go to the toy department and look at all the toys. It seemed that most stores had a toy section in order to keep the children away from their mothers while they shopped. I did not think much of a store if they did not have a toy department. Sometimes Mother would give me a few coins to buy something.

Up the street from us was the post office. I would save my pennies and dimes and go with Mother and buy saving stamps and put them in a book. The stamps cost ten cents each. When I got enough stamps, I could trade them in for a twenty-five-dollar war bond. I remember the book with all the stamps in it but I don't remember getting enough stamps to get a real bond. Of course, growing up during the Second World War and buying savings bonds and having a victory garden was expected of everyone. I guess that was why we had a garden behind our house on the railroad's property.

A lasting memory was that walking downtown we would see flags in people's windows with some kind of stars on them that indicated that they had a son in the service or one killed in the war. It is not clear in my mind how these flags and stars were laid out but many had them. I can remember my parents commenting on the people they knew who had lost children or relative in the war and how sad they were for these families. My mother's youngest brother uncle Milton was in the Army during the Second World War. I remember seeing him in his Army uniform and how impressed I was to see him in his uniform. The family seemed to look up to him for serving in the army. The other family member that I knew was in the war was Kenney Hydrick who was Daddy's

49

nephew by his sister Thelma. He was in one of those long marches in the Philippians and came out of the service shell shocked and never was the same after that. He always seemed sad and moved slowly. He was a good carpenter but always had a sad air about him.

Outside of Aiken was a prisoner of war camp. I can remember riding by on the way to Marion's house and seeing all those men behind fences like so many cows. I don't think I will ever forget this. I was told that many of the German prisoners of war let it be known that after the war they were going to come back and settle in Aiken and marry a southern girl. As far as I know none of them ever came back. But, who knows, some may have come back.

Also, on the way to Marion's house was Daddy's Lions Clubhouse. Daddy was very active in the Lions Club and I can remember going to the clubhouse with him from time to time. I am pretty sure that he was president of the club for one term or had some other type of leadership position. Sometime during my youth in Aiken, Daddy became District Governor of the Lions Club. One of the highlights while he was District Governor, that Daddy often talked about, was a trip he and Mother took to Havana, Cuba on a District Governor's convention. It must have been a once in a life time trip because he talked about this trip the rest of his life.

It seems that on the way to Marion's house we passed where my grandfather

on my mother's side was buried. Later on, after we moved to Edisto, my grandmother was buried there also. My grandfather died before I was born. Because of this I never knew him and know very little about him. But I can remember going with Mother and Daddy to his grave. About all I knew about him was that I was told he was a very successful cotton broker before the depression and went broke after the depression. My mother often talked about the good times before the depression and the hard times after the depression. About all I was told about my grandmother on this side of the family is that she loved to grow flowers and had mother constantly going out to the barnyard and getting cow mature for her flower garden. My mother also grew many flowers and I have around 100 camellias. Maybe these likes for this or that are handed down.

As far back as I can remember we went to church every Sunday at the Methodist Church which was not far from the movie house where we went to see Roy Rogers. I can still remember learning how to sing Jesus loves me this I know for the Bible tells me so. It seems like most of our activities outside of home were around the church or around Mother's large family and my many cousins.

Another fond memory was going to Uncle George's and Uncle Ed's feed and seed store on Main Street across from the movie house in downtown Aiken. There were rows and rows of bins with all kind of seeds and bags of stuff. I did not know what was in them. I loved to just go around and run my hands through the seed in the bins. No one seemed to mind and I just wandered around until Mother and Daddy were ready to go. I always thought Uncle Ed was funny. He was a small man who walked around bent over because of some kind of back problem. It did not seem to bother him because he was always laughing and cutting up. Uncle George was more serious.

Every now and then we would go to Augusta to shop or go to the doctor. I always loved riding through Aiken with its divided streets and then coming to a wide-open road to Augusta. The road always seemed bigger than the roads around Aiken. On the way to Augusta from Aiken there were hills that the highway had cut through and little business here and there. We also had to cross the Savannah River to get to Augusta. At that time Augusta was a quaint town much like Aiken. I recently went to Augusta on business and it had lost its quaintness and seemed more like a maze with all its four lane highways going here and there. But when I was coming up in Aiken the trip to Augusta was a pleasant one. As I grow older, largeness and people going aimlessly here and there is not a pleasant experience. This is one reason I love Edisto. It has not yet become overrun with people going here and there for no apparent reason.

On the street to downtown from our house you bad to pass a large church, the Court House and a funeral home on our side of the street. At the end of the street before it turned to go to the two-block business section was the post office with a large statue in the middle of the road. I don't remember what kind of statue it was. I mention this because it was a fascinating walk for a young curious boy to take. All kinds of things went through my bead as I walked this short distance. At the time it seemed like a long way. From time to time I have gone back to Aiken and everything looked smaller than I envisioned as a young child growing up there.

This was an innocent time but yet a turbulent time in the nation's history. There was a war going on and everyone was expected to do bis part. It seemed like I did not know anyone that did not work bard and I never heard of any crime and was not concerned with walking downtown by myself nor was my mother. Things were not very costly and money did not seem to be a problem, at least for our family. We bad plenty to eat and a warm house in a pleasant neighborhood. Nowadays living by a railroad track may not be so desirable but I thought it was wonderful to be able to often see the large steam engines coming by my house just puffing and puffing.

I feel blessed to have had the opportunity to come up in such an exciting and yet innocent time. The standards we lived by were clear and those that did not live up to Biblical standards were shunned and considered less than desirable people to be around. I guess society back then just expected more out of their citizens and by expecting more they got the best from most people.

Ob, I bad one uncle that spent two years in prison for stealing money from the company he worked for. The family was so ashamed of him that they told all the kids that he bad TB and was going to be in the hospital for the next two years to get well. I only found out the truth about 30 years later at a family funeral. My Aunt Ruth got several of the second generation together and told us some of the family secrets. So, I guess everything was not as innocent as it seemed when I was growing up.

As I have already related, we spent the summers from 1942 to 1947 on Edisto

Beach to get Mother away from her older brothers and all that was going on in her family. Things did not get better so Daddy permanently moved the family to Edisto Beach in the fall of 1947. Daddy told everyone be was moving to Edisto for my health. In fact, I thought this was the reason we moved to Edisto for a long time until I began to put things together and figured out the real reason. I believe Daddy even told my younger brother when he was up in age all about why be moved to Edisto.

The next chapter will be about Mother's brothers and sisters and Daddy's brothers and sisters. After that I will try to record all I know about the Lybrand family tree from as far back as I can go to the present.

I have enjoyed reliving my childhood; I hope you have. It would be nice for your future children if you would start a general log or diary on the major events in your life for your future children and grandchildren that you can continue where I have left off.

God bless you, every one of you.

**Old pictures tell more than just words**

The following are some old pictures taken in Aiken, SC before we moved to Edisto Beach, SC.

1st Cousins Helen & Jo Ellen & Me
In our back yard in Aiken, SC

Sammie Lybrand

Aiken School picture
of Me

Sammie Lybrand

Left to right: Pictures of our house in Aiken, Backyard - Mother sitting on side yard with me and Tom - Me sitting on steps from back yard to street - Back of house from side yard. Not sure of people - Front of house looking at carport - Tom & Me

Pictures of Granny from left to right
taken at our house at 1441 Park Ave.

Granny near carport
Granny on Front side walk- Note park across the street.
Granny near steps from back yard to street in front of our house.

Pictures of my Mother - Some early on

<u>Top left</u> - Mother on down-Town Aiken, SC street.

<u>Top Right</u> - Mother with Tom and me and Aunt Mildred.

<u>Bottom left</u> - Early swim suits - Mother second from left.

<u>Middle</u> - Early picture of Mother about the time she Was married

# Chapter Two



Isaiah: 6:8 KJV

*Also, I heard the voice of the Lord, saying, Whom shall I send and who will go for us? Then said I, Here am I; send me.*

In this chapter I will try to tell you a little bit about my father's brother and sisters and also a little bit about my mother's brothers and sisters. I have a little bit about my mother's ancestors that I will include. This book is being written so that you will know something about your ancestral line. You can pick up where I have left off if you want to know more about your extended family. One interesting point is that if my grandchildren tried to trace all their ancestors back the 16 generations this book covers, they would have to check out 120,000 grandparents. This is the reason I have only covered my direct line with a few exceptions.

As I go through the brothers and sisters of Daddy's and Mother's I will put what dates I have. The first date will be when they were born and the second date will be when they died. If I do not have the date they died I will just put an asterisk. I have listed my first cousins to show how many I had. I have not tried to put dates beside their names. If I know that they have died I will also put an asterisk by their names. As of 2012 all of Daddy's and Mother's brothers and sisters and their spouses have died. Daddy and Aunt Doughty were the last to die in this whole bunch.

As I go through these relatives, I will try to give you where they lived and what they did for a living.

**Daddy's side:**

Daddy had one brother and two sisters that lived to adulthood. They were Thelma, Sue, and Jack. He had a sister named Essie that was born on August 30, 1900 and died on December 5, 1900.

His parents were:
**John Samuel Lybrand**-May 3, 1872 November 28, 1924
**Mamie Louise Clayton** -July 7, 1878 - March 16, 1973


**Thelma Jane Lybrand** - September 26, 1901 and died May 5, 1927 during the birth of her fifth child.
She married **Fred Quitman Hydrick** *
They had **Rhett Elmore Hydrick** *
**Ray Philip Hydrick** (He is over 90 years old in 2012)
**Kenneth Earl Hydrick** *
**Frances Louise Hydrick**


I know very little about Thelma. Daddy would often say that she regularly beat up on him and Jack. Daddy said that his Mother told her that she had better be nice to them because one of these days they would grow up and beat up on her. She died one year after Daddy graduated from college.


**Harvie Samuel Lybrand** - August 3, 1904 - November 25, 1997
He married **Jennie Brown Owens**-March 4, 1910-January 6,1987
They had **Thomas Harvie Lybrand** *
**George Samuel Lybrand** (Me)
**David Ladson Lybrand**
You now know more than most people know about their grandfather and great grandfather.


**Charlie Clayton {Jack) Lybrand** - Feb. 24, 1908 *
He married **Erna Gertrude Butler** - May 19, 1910 *
They had **Louisa Erna Lybrand** * (Only lived a short time,)
**Charlie Clayton Lybrand, Jr.**

Uncle Jack worked for a downtown Ford dealership in Charleston, SC as an automobile front end alignment specialist. I remember going to see him at work and he was down in a hole under a car working on its alignment. He and Aunt Erna lived in the smallest house I ever saw. People called it a mill house. It had a small living room, eat in kitchen, two bedrooms and one bath. I spent at least one night with them and Uncle Jack literally rocked the house snoring. His snoring was the loudest I have ever heard before or since. Later on, he built a large den off the back of the house. He built a pretty white picket fence around the house out of wooden boxes he saved from work. But you could not tell they were built out of scrap lumber. Uncle Jack seemed happy all the time and was fun to be around.

**Susie {Sue) Lybrand** - November 3, 1910 - 1987
She married **Jack William Smithson*** (Married a short time.)
**Charles Robert Parker**

Sue moved to Charleston, SC to work for the Navy Yard. Grandmother moved down to live with her after she had lived with us in Aiken. Frances also moved down to Charleston to live with Sue. As I have previously mentioned Sue and Frances lived in a rented house in North Charleston, SC. While they were living in North Charleston Frances met and married a sailor and moved to New Mexico. The next place we visited Sue and Granny was in government housing or tenements as they were called. They were brick and there were multiple units in one building. Later Sue bought her own house in North Charleston. Granny died while they were living in this house. Sue later died while living in this house. She had married Charles Parker and they were living in Sue's house when she died. Sue did not get married until after she was 50 years old and was married twice before she was 60 years old. Before marrying Charles, she married Navy Chief Jack Smithson. Sadly, he only lived a few years after they were married.

While visiting Granny in this house I noticed that Granny had a bottle of her medicine sitting on the windowsill above the sink. Daddy would often bring her a pint of bourbon. Granny would take the bourbon and pour it into her bottle of medicine and place a sassafras root in it and call it "Acidity." Every night she would take a large tablespoon of her medicine to help her sleep. It must have been good for her because she lived to 95 and I do not remember her being sick very much during her life. Granny was a small lady but extremely active. When she was in her mid-eighties, she made the statement that if she was 65 again, she would have an acre garden,

There is one story she told me. When she was a teenager her appendix broke and she almost died because she could not keep anything she ate down. One day her mother was cooking greens and they smelled so good to her. She asked her mother to give her a cup of the green's liquor and she began to sip it and was able to keep it down. Therefore, after that she bit by bit got her strength back.

When Granny died Mother and Daddy worried how Sue would get by because Granny waited on her hand and foot. Shortly after Granny died, we went to eat a meal with Sue and the food tasted just like Granny would cook. Mother looked at Sue and asked her how she did it since Granny had just died and she had not had enough time to learn how to cook. Sue looked at Mother and said, "Do you think I am blind? I've been watching Granny for years and just did what she did."

Daddy' s immediate family was rather small compared to Mother's. But later in life I found out that he had around 60 first cousins that I had never met. His grandfather, GW or George Washington Lybrand, had at least eight children that I know about and all of these had a bunch of children. I am not sure how many children Granny's family had or even their names. The reason we did not go back to the New Holland and Lexington area is because we always went to see Granny in Charleston. When I lived in Lexington, I could have tried to meet some of these close relatives but did not know how to start. Since I started this book, I have met several of Daddy's first cousins who have helped contribute to this book. I have identified what they contributed.

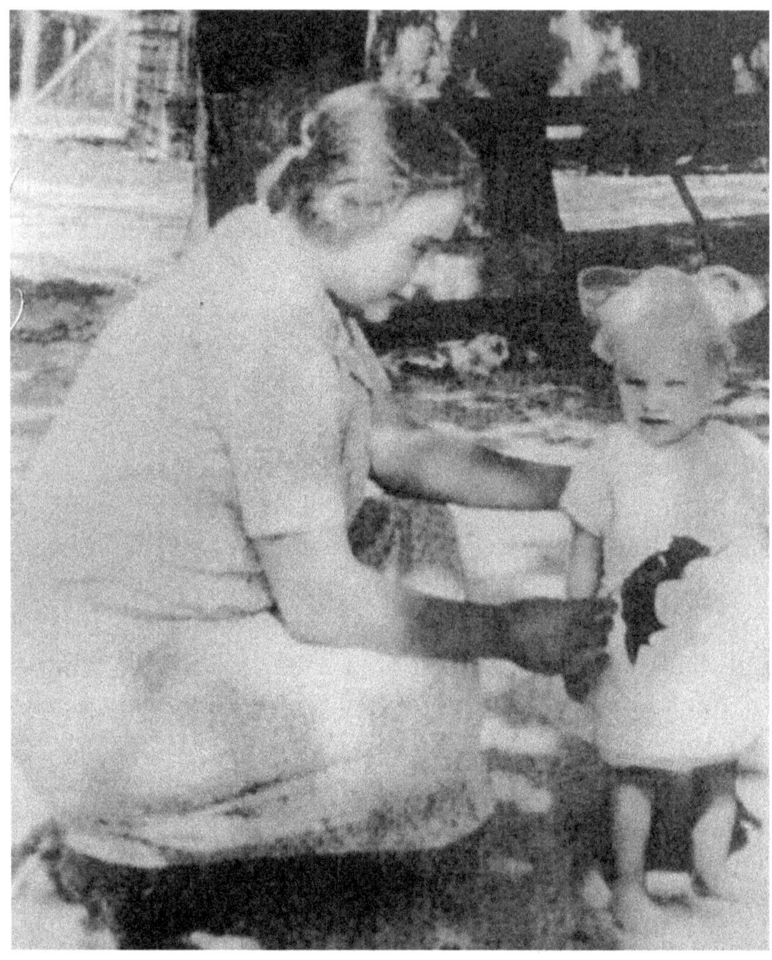

The picture to the left is a long-lost picture of Thelma who died in child birth with her fifth child. The child is believed to be Frances.

The next page is of the rest of Daddy's family in the 1970s. From left to right: Daddy, Mother, Jack (Sue's husband), Sue, Granny, Jack and Erna.

**Mother's side:**

Mother was born into a large family that lived in Aiken. She had eight brothers and sisters that lived. She had a sister that died at an

63

early age. Starting with the oldest they were Myrtle, Florence, Lenwood, Ruth, Bessie, George, Ed, Jennie, Doughty and Milton. Let me tell you a little bit about them. For years everyone was expected to come to a yearly family reunion. You were given a hard time if you did not show up at all the family reunions. These reunions were rotated among the bothers' or sisters' homes. It seems that over my childhood we must have had a reunion at every uncle's or aunt's house. Sometimes Aunt Bessie had her turn in Aiken because she lived so far away. Maybe Aunt Doughty had her turn in Aiken also. As I remember, Bessie and Doughty held their reunions in an Aiken church hall. As the years have gone on, these reunions have become less frequent because many of my cousins' families have become large and they are now having their own get togethers.

Mother's parents were **George Edmund Owens** - March 22, 1869 - May 23, 1929   **Dora Sovereign Bates** - June 1, 1876 - December 6, 1948

They were married December 26, 1894.

<u>Mother's brothers and sisters are listed below.</u>

**Harriet Myrtle Owens-**_November 30, 1895 *

She Married Leon Champion Eubanks, Jr. - Sept. 28, 1892 - March 23, 1960

They had **Leon Champion Eubanks** *

**Ruth Eubanks**

**George Edmond Eubanks** (Buddy) *

**Marion Eubanks**

Aunt Myrtle and Uncle Leon lived outside of Aiken on a dairy farm. They lived in an old farm house similar to Granny's house with an outside privy and wash basin on the back porch. I loved to go visit them and see all the farm animals. As I got older Marion and I would walk all over their farm exploring. I remember it being beautiful with its rolling hills covered with pastures full of cattle. A couple of funny family stories that were told over and over at family reunions were about Leon. It seemed that he was always getting in trouble and his sister Ruth sort of picked on him. One day he was out in the barnyard and tripped and his false teeth flew out of his mouth and landed in fresh cow manure. Ruth related that he must have washed his false teeth a hundred times before he would put them back in his mouth. Another one was that Leon was helping his mother and Ruth in the kitchen cutting up onions and the onion smell got in his eyes so bad that he started crying and asked for a wet cloth to clean out his eyes. Ruth handed him a wet diaper. He used it awhile and when he realized what he was using, he threw it at her.

**Florence Owens** * November 20, 1897 and died November 15. 1902
> **Joseph Lenwood Owens** - April 2, 1899 *
>> He married **Annye Clyde Montgomery** - January 15, 1905 *
>> They had **Sara Lenette Owens**
>> **Ned Montgomery Owens**

Uncle Lenwood and Aunt Clyde also lived on a dairy farm in Milledgeville, Georgia. I am not sure but I believe it was owned by Aunt Clyde's family. I only remember visiting there once coming up. One time while I was visiting Aunt Doughty in Athens, GA two of her boys, Bob and Owens and I went hunting on their land. Their farm seemed to be large because we stayed out in their fields for quite some time.

**Ruth Alice Owens** - September 3, 1900 *
She married **John Lawton Bell** - 1892 *
The had **John Edmund Bell** *
> **Anna Mary Bell** *
> **Jane Bell**

Uncle John and Aunt Ruth were my favorites. They lived on land grant property outside of Orangeburg, SC inherited by Uncle John. Aunt Ruth worked as a social worker and started several social programs in South Carolina and Uncle John stayed home. Their agreement was that she would make the money and he would feed them. He had a large vegetable garden, a couple of pigs, a cow and a pond from which he got fish. They had a large muscadine arbor for wine and jam. He always had peanuts that he raised. If you wanted peanuts Uncle John would go pull up several peanut plants that had hundreds of peanuts attached to their roots. He then would shell the peanuts and parch them. He would always tell you to eat until you were satisfied. You name it and he had it growing. I loved to go stay with them because Uncle John always had time to go fishing with you or go hunting with you. Aunt Ruth had a rule that anything you killed you had to eat. One time I killed a blue jay and a bull frog. I had to clean them both and that night I had a fried bluejay and fried frog legs. By the time I came along and visited Aunt Ruth her children. had already grown up and had left home.

**Bessie Gertrude Owens** - September 16, 1902 *
She married **Wilson Burnson Causey** - August 21, 1904 *
They adopted **Wilson Edmund Causey** (Billy)
**George Robert Causey** (Bobby)

Aunt Bessie and Uncle Wilson lived in Cocoa, Florida. The first time I remember visiting them, they lived on Merritt Island on the Indian River with lots of fruit trees around them. I remember going in their back yard and picking tangerines and eating all I wanted. Not long after that they had to sell their property to the government and move into town because the government was going to build the Cape Canaveral Space Center on their property. Uncle Wilson was a government fruit inspector. He would go around to fruit shipping centers and make sure the fruit was good enough to ship. I remember he carried a very long, very sharp, thin pocket knife that he used to cut open fruit to inspect it. I went around with him several times. One time when I was stationed in Miami, Florida with the Coast Guard and was on my way to Charleston, my car's alternator went out right outside of Cocoa. I called Uncle Wilson and he got a mechanic he knew to tow my car in and replace the alternator. I had to spend the night. That afternoon I rode around with Uncle Wilson who was a right fat person, as was Aunt Bessie. One thing that impressed me that afternoon was that Uncle Wilson rode all over town looking for chocolate covered marshmallows on some kind of cracker. That evening after supper Uncle Wilson and Aunt Bessie sat in lounge chairs in front of the TV eating these special crackers Uncle Wilson had searched for all over town. The next morning my car was fixed and I was on my way again. I guess it is good to have relatives all over the country.

**George McDonald Owens** - April 9, 1904 *
He married **Ruby Lenora Leach** - September 16, 1915 *
They had **Charlotte Joallen Owens** (Jo Ellen)*
**Helen Elizabeth Owens**
**Mildred Claire Owens** (Claire)*
**Georgia Lynn Owens**
**Ruby Lenora Owens** (Lenora)

Uncle George and Aunt Ruby lived in Aiken and had a house full of girls. Aunt Ruby was from Augusta, Maine. I am not sure of the connection or how he met her. I often played with Helen and Jo Ellen while we were in Aiken because they were about my same age. They also lived close to us. I remember either Uncle George or Uncle Ed lived in a log cabin and we visited them often. Uncle George and Uncle Ed seem to go together because they worked together running a feed and seed store and moving large trees for the northerners that came to Aiken, SC for the racing season. It seemed when you mentioned one you mentioned the other like George and Ed did this or did that. Later they bought a farm out on Whiskey Road and started a nursery. Uncle George particularly liked camellias and discovered a unique seedling which named

Miss Aiken. It has won many camellia shows over the years. I have a Miss Aiken that came from a cutting from the original plant. In 2009 I won "Best Local Bloom" in the Coastal Carolina Camellia Society show in Charleston, SC with my Miss Aiken. Joyce and I are members of this society.

**Robert Edmund Owens** - January 23, 1906 *
He married **Mildred Lillian Tyler** - March 31, 1914 *
They adopted **Robert Edmund Owens, Jr.** (Bobby) *
**Mildred Catherine Owens** (Catherine)

Uncle Ed was always bent over from some kind of back problem. He was affectionately called "Uncie Boy." I am not certain of the spelling of "Uncie". He worked right along with his brother in their several businesses. I played with Bobby along with Helen and Jo Ellen because Uncle Ed and Aunt Mildred also lived in Aiken. He was always joking around. But it was he and Uncle George that gave Mother a hard time with Tommie while Daddy was off selling school books. I tell people if it were not for George and Ed we would still be in Aiken. Uncle Ed was the first to die and the funeral home up the street from us on Park Avenue handled the funeral. I was fairly young when he died. I remember walking over to Uncle Ed's casket and looking in at him when several grownups came over at the same time and pressed me against the casket. It made me get up real close to Uncle Ed lying there and I almost panicked until I could squirm away. To this day I have a phobia that I cannot look at dead bodies, even people close to me. I seem to panic just looking at dead bodies up close in a casket.

**Jennie Brown Owens** - March 4, 1910 - June 6, 1987 * My Mother
She Married **Harvie Samuel Lybrand**-August 2, 1904-Nov.25, 1997
The got married in 1932.
They had **Thomas Harvie Lybrand** *
**George Samuel Lybrand** - Me
**David Ladson Lybrand**

By now you probably know more about my father and me than you know about most of your kin. About the only thing I want to add is that after we moved to Edisto and Mother was settled in, from time to time we went back to Aiken to visit Mother's kin folks. Daddy's favorite thing to do was to beat George and Ed at "Pennyante" or penny poker. He got the biggest kick out of beating them and taking all their money at poker. With penny poker you could not lose much but to end up a game with piles of pennies was pure joy to Daddy. I guess they had caused him so much trouble over time that he just liked getting back at them in a friendly way. Daddy did tell me that right after he and Mother got married George and Ed chained their car between two trucks and paraded them down town blowing their horns and then let them go at the other end of town.

One thing that I think is worth telling is that in Mother's last couple of years she became anemic and she received B-12 shots for the anemia. This went on for a long time. The doctor finally had her x-rayed to see if there was anything wrong with her brain and found nothing. I remember being in her hospital room and the doctor coming in and telling us that there was absolutely nothing wrong with her brain to cause her to become so weak. Shortly after that I clearly remember leaving her hospital room to go home and her calling me Bessie and everyone around her Bessie. The doctors then realized that there was something wrong with her brain. A closer survey revealed a large tumor down in her brain that would not have shown up on a regular x-ray. This was what had been causing the anemia all along and probably had been growing for several years. They tried radiation treatments but they did not work. She lost all ability to communicate and died shortly thereafter.


**Dora Bates Owens** - August 19, 1912 *    (Her nickname was Doughty.)

She married **Ralph Vincent Smith** - September 15, 1909 *
The had **Ralph Vincent Smith, Jr.** *

**Robert Brown Smith** (Bob)
**Joseph Owens Smith** (Owensy)
**Carolyn Anne Smith** (Anne)
**Phillip Cameron Smith**
**James Hilton Smith** (Jim)

Aunt Doughty and Uncle Ralph lived in Gaffney, SC originally. He was a baker and she taught school. When their children got older, they realized that they could not afford to send them all to college. Therefore, they looked around for a college town where they both could find employment and moved to Athens, Georgia where the University of Georgia was. All of their children graduated from the University of Georgia. Uncle Ralph continued in the bakery business and Aunt Doughty taught business courses on the college level. Later they ran a nursery on the property they bought outside of Athens. I visited them several times in Athens and roamed the woods around Athens hunting with Bob and Owensy. Aunt Doughty was my mother's favorite sibling and she visited her as often as she could. When Daddy retired, he wanted to travel the world but Mother would not go with him. Daddy complained because she would travel eight hours to see Aunt Doughty and would not travel a few hours on an airplane with him to visit some of the world. Daddy eventually just joined group tours and went by himself.

**Milton Owens**-October 18. 1914 *
> He married **Vera Golden** - January 26, 1919 *
> They had **Milton Owens, Jr**. *

Uncle Milton and Aunt Vera lived in Winter Haven, Florida. He was also a fruit inspector. I believe Uncle Wilson got him the job. Aunt Vera was from Hampton, South Carolina. Their son, who they called "Little Milton" was killed in 1955 or 1956 in a gun accident. I remember his death because I was a freshman at The Citadel and was asked to be a pallbearer. He was only ten years old. It seems that he was visiting a neighborhood boy, whose father was a policeman. The friend found his father's gun and was showing it to Little Milton and pulled the trigger and blew his heart out. Uncle Milton and Aunt Vera never really got over his death and never had any more children. Not long before Aunt Vera died, she was still talking about Little Milton as if he had just died. When Uncle Milton died, I was also asked to be a pallbearer. At the time of Uncle Milton's death, it seems that Aunt Vera was in the hospital and when she got ready to come home, she called Uncle Milton to come get her. She waited and waited on him and eventually called a friend to come get her. When she got home Uncle Milton was not there. They began looking for him and found him in the hospital's parking lot slumped over dead in his car.

I have a little sketchy information about my mother's ancestors. The following information came from a handwritten sketch and all the names were not clear. Therefore, this is the best I can do with what I had to deal with.

### Dora Bates (My Mother's mother)

| Sovereign Bates | Harriette Haseltine Johnson |
| :---: | :---: |
| I | I |
| Jessie Bates - Whittie Bryant | John Johnson  Rebecca Heath |

### George Edmund Owens (My Mother's Father)

| George MacDonald Owens | Kizanna Toole |
| :---: | :---: |
| I | I |
| Edmund Owens  Thiss Wood | Stephen Toole  Griss Sanders |

Several times at family reunions Aunt Doughty told of Moms' (As she called her mother) mother, Harriette Johnson, waiting and waiting for her father to come home from the Civil War. She related that it was common after the Civil War to see many men walking home down the road that went past their farm. Many were in bad shape. Some would stop and ask for food and to rest a bit. They would take them in and feed them with what little they had because they were short of everything after the Civil War. They did this hoping that some good people would do the same for their father that was also walking home from the Civil War. On one occasion a beat up ragged man came to the door and just walked in as if he lived there. They did not recognize him as their father and asked what he was doing. He said in a weak voice, "Don't you recognize me, Mom?" They all fell on him and welcomed him home and started trying to nurse him back to health. But he did not regain his strength and died a year or so later.

I hope that you have noticed that going through all this there are many names of people that have contributed to your genes. In the next chapter many more names will be added to those people that have contributed to your gene pool. This book is primarily about the Lybrand clan but in reality, there are hundreds if not thousands of people in your past family history that have contributed to your blood line. Therefore, be kind to everyone you see because if you go back a little bit you may find that you are kin to them. Some of the relatives I have met over the years led me to believe that we may truly have some monkeys in our ancestry.

As I have said before, it is my desire that all of you keep a diary of special family events so you can pass the Lybrand family history down to our future generations.

## John 1:1-5 KJV

*In the beginning was the Word, and the Word was with God, and the Word was God.*

*The same was in the beginning with God.*

*All things were made by Him; and without Him was not anything made that was made.*

*In Him was life; and the life was the light of men.*

*And the light shineth in darkness; and the darkness comprehended it not.*

The following are some pictures of Mother's large family. I have also included a Coat-of-Arms of the Owens that came from Aunt Vera's final effects. Aunt Vera's niece, Mickey Garvin, gave it to me to hand down to the descendants of the Owens. Aunt Vera went to live with her brother, Neil Golden (Mickey's father), in Hollywood, SC after Uncle Milton died. She died about five years after she went to live with her brother.

Top: Mother's mother Dora Sovereign Bates. - Bottom: Aunt Ruth, Aunt Bessie, Mother, Aunt Doughty. Taken in Aug, 1981

The next page has two pictures of Mother's family. The first picture has all of Mother's family. I will try to identify each of them from left to right starting at the bottom of the picture.

**Top Picture:**

### First Row

Little Milton, Uncle Milton's and Aunt Vera's son who died around 1955. Therefore, this picture had to be taken around 1954.

### Second Row

My mother; Katherine Owens, Uncle Ed Daughter; Aunt Vera, Uncle Milton, Aunt Doughty and Uncle Ralph.

### Third Row

My Daddy, Uncle Ed, Aunt Mildred, Aunt Ruth, Uncle John; Helen Owens, Uncle George Daughter.

### Fourth Row

Aunt Bessie, Uncle Wilson, Uncle Leon, Aunt Myrtle, Aunt Ruby, Uncle George.

### Fifth Row

Uncle Lenwood, Aunt Clyde; Bobby Owens, Uncle Ed's son; Buddy Eubanks, Aunt Myrtle's son; and Marion Eubanks, Aunt Myrtle's son.

This picture appeared in the Aiken Standard newspaper and had the following to say about this picture

(Photo by Quattlebaum Studio, Aiken, S. C.)

Shown here are the direct descendants of the late Mr. and Mrs. G. E. Owens who came from three states to be present at the recent sesquicentennial home coming at the First Baptist Church, Aiken. They are, first row, left to right: Mrs. Harvie Lybrand of Edisto Beach; Katherine Owens, Aiken; Mrs. Milton Owens, Milton, Jr., Mr. Owens, Sr., Hampton; Mrs. Ralph Smith, and Mr. Smith. Athens, Ga. Second row, left to right: Harvie Lybrand, Edisto Beach; Ed Owens. and Mrs. Owens, Aiken; Mrs. John Lawton Bell, Mr. Bell, Orangeburg. Third row, left to right: Helen Owens, Aiken; Mrs. W. B. Causey and Mr. Causey, Cocoa, Florida. Fourth row, left to right: Mrs. J. L. Owens and Mr. Owens, Milledgeville, Ga.; Mr. and Mrs. L. C. Eubanks, Aiken; Mrs. George Owens, and Mr. Owens, Aiken; fifth row, left to right: Robert Owens, Edmund Eubanks, and Marion Eubanks, Aiken.—*Reporter*

Bottom Picture: (This picture was taken at the 1981 Ownes Family Reunion in Aiken, SC.) From Left to right: Uncle Ralph, Aunt Doughty, Aunt Mildred, Aunt Ruby, Uncle George, Aunt Bessie, Aunt Vera, Uncle Milton, Mother, Daddy.

HONESTAS OPTIMA POLITIA
Owens

# Chapter THREE



*But they that wait upon the Lord shall renew their strength; they shall mount up with wings as eagles; they shall run, and not be weary; and they shall walk, and not faint.*

My children and grandchildren and maybe soon to be great grandchildren, lend me your ear. Like it or not, the past determines the lot we are given to live out the time that is ordained by God for us to live. Our line might have died out and we would not be living this day if one of our grandparents had ten children and three died and our line was determined by one of those that died. If you had been in one of these deadlines you would not be here to read this Lybrand story. But if your line came from one of the children that lived you are alive to read this Lybrand story. Therefore, you had nothing to do with your birth and who your parents are. It is not what happens to you, it is what you do with what hand you are dealt. I was born sickly, had a serious heart by-pass in 1988, your grandmother Ida was sick for seven years with lupus and died in 2000 leaving me broke and owning nothing. Then in 2004 I was told I had a five percent or less chance of living because I had pancreatic cancer. My attitude during all this was to get on with what I faced and to make the best of it. As a result, it is 2012 and I am writing you a history of your clan so that you will have a strong feeling of where you came from and what may lie ahead. On the bright side, after my first wife, Ida, died I was fortunate enough to come back home to Edisto and marry Joyce, a nice lady I grew up with and dated a little. We got married in late 2000 and have enjoyed each other's company ever since.

As far as I can determine, you came from a strong people who loved God and lived as close to His commandments as humanly possible. As far as I can determine, they are a friendly bunch and easy to talk to. So, stand tall because the Lybrand's are a great people and one you can be proud to descend from.

In the 1700s the first Lybrand came from Germany to the midlands of South Carolina to an area called Saxe Gotha, later called the Lexington area. There was turmoil in Europe with princes and kings constantly fighting over the control of the area. One could not rest easy because he did not know if someone knocking on his door was a friend or someone to take him off and kill him or take what little he had. Therefore, many Germans came to America to get away from all this turmoil and the promise of free land.

In the meantime, the east coast of America was being settled and there was a fight going on among the English, French and Spanish as to who was going to control this area. During this time the English had established Charles Town. The English were concerned about the Indians and French in the upstate area of South Carolina and wanted a buffer between Charles Town and the Indians.

The English king at the time had a German heritage and began offering Germans and other European peasants and tradesmen free land in the upstate if they would come to Charles Town and get a land grant. Usually the amount of each land grant was 50 acres per person in a family. Some reports I have read said they were offered 100 acres for the head of household and an extra 50 acres for each additional family member. They were even offered a bounty or money to get started clearing land and to build a shelter to live in. In some cases, even the trip over was paid for. There are many differing accounts of what incentives these peasants were offered to come help settle the upcountry of South Carolina. Many came and your ancestors were among those that came. From what I have read the first Lybrand family that came were brick masons.

The majority of those that came from Germany came down the Rhine River to Rotterdam and caught a sailing ship to Charles Town. Some accounts tell that the trip over took about three months and the conditions aboard were bad to say the least. The passengers had little space and even had to take turns sleeping on a single cot. The space they were allotted was very small and tempers flared among the passengers because of the limited space. Some got sick and some even died on the crossing. Frequent Atlantic storms made the trip miserable and many got seasick. For a whole family to make the crossing alive sometimes seemed like a miracle. But when land was finally sighted all the hardships seem to disappear.

When they arrived, the ships were met. Those that had paid their way got busy and started the process of claiming the land grants they were promised. Those that had not paid their way were indentured for several years to pay for their passages. Tradesmen were especially sought as indentured servants. The first Lybrand that came to this country was Hendrick Lybrand. According to the account I have, he came to Charles Town and had paid for his passage and his family's passage from Rotterdam to Charles Town.

Once the land grant was given, a surveyor was given the task of laying out the allotted plot for each family. The trip to the upcountry is another story. They had three ways of getting to the area of their allotted land grant. First, they could go by water because rivers go from Charleston to the midlands. Second, they could go by wagon train that provided protection in numbers from the Indians. Or, if they had the money, they would go by stage coach. My guess is that they went by wagon train because they had to have taken supplies and tools to quickly establish shelters from themselves and their families. But I have no proof or information on how they got to their land.

Once they got to the area, the surveyor laid out their allotted land grant next to or above the last land grant issued. Therefore, the plat they were given had boundaries that showed that some sides of their land grant were next to the previous person that got a land grant, etc. The plats also show vacant land boundaries where the next person was going to get his land.

What I want you to take away from this account is that it was no small feat by your first ancestor that came to America. He had to pull up roots and come to an unknown land to seek a new life where he could be awarded for the labor of his family and himself without someone coming and taking it away from him without recourse.

The thing that struck me the most was that once Hendrick Lybrand and his family boarded the ship, landed in Charles Town and headed to his land grant, there was no turning back. Whether or not the land grant he got and the surrounding area was to his liking he was stuck and he had to make the best of it. It was a live or die situation. If he did not like what he found he could not get on a bus and go back to Germany. I guess his situation in Germany was bad enough that he and his family were willing to endure anything to have the opportunity to start over and to build a new life that would last for generations. His dream has come true because his descendants are still alive and prospering. I am one of his descendants alive and recording his story.

A strong belief in Jesus Christ was brought with your ancestors and they helped initiate four strong churches over time. I even have my grandfather's and my mother's Bibles. God has been with the Lybrand family though all these generations I am about to tell you about.

Be thankful that, at least from your Lybrand kin, you have received strong and determined traits to achieve and to do the best you can in life with what God has given you to work with.

**Rabbit Trail:**

## Something to think about

My children and grandchildren, when working on our ancestry, I actually only consider the family name that we currently have. As you can see from the chart below, as each generation goes by, we accumulate twice as many grandparents as the generation before. This search of the Lybrand's only goes back 16 generations. At 16 generations Samuel Dupree and John Daniel Hay Lybrand (plus my other grandchildren) would have approximately 120,000 actual grandparents. If they can extend it to 17 generations, they would have around 240,000 grandparents, etc. Of course, we must consider the women that married into the Lybrand clan. We also have the genes of these ladies inherited in our gene pool. If you tried to follow all these lines provided by our grandmothers it would take a lifetime and you'd probably never finish in one lifetime. Here is a list of those grandmothers I could identify. They are Marie (no last name known), Baerkler, Margaretha (no last name known), Weiss, (Christian's wife is not known), Benay, Fulmer, Derrick, Jackson, Clayton, Owens, and Myers. From your grandmother Ida you also have Harley and Knight. On my mother's side you would also have to consider Bates, Bryant, Johnson, Heath, Wood, Toole and Sanders. That amounts to about 20 family last names I can identify. You could take any of these names and search them back as I have searched the Lybrand name back and you would eventually come to your generation. If Samuel Dupree Lybrand, Jimmy's son, really wanted to find out all he is kin to, he could take any of these names mentioned and search them back as far as he could. As I just mentioned, if he followed all of his ancestors back it would take a lifetime and then he probably would not get finished. There is no telling what he would come across, good or bad. In one of my searches I found out that President Jimmy Carter's wife was kin to the Lybrand's. When I tried to figure out how she was kin, I gave up because it went back too many generations with too many names. This is just an example of what you might find.

I am going to tell you several times in this book to start keeping a diary of major family events and all funny and unusual events and when you get a little older start writing your own book that takes up where this book leaves off. I would love to know more about the people listed below than what I have recorded in this book. Even little details would make them come alive.

## The numbers of your Grandparents

*(Note that Laken, Anne, James, Robert and Sarah are in generation one. The girls will eventually have different last names if they get married and James and Robert will keep the King name. They are still in the Lybrand*

*line and may eventually have different names. But they are as important to me as Samuel Dupree and John Daniel Lybrand are.)*

| Generation | # Grandparents In Generation | Total# Grandparents | Name of Descendant |
|---|---|---|---|
| 1 | 2 | 2 | *Samuel Dupree Lybrand |
| 1 | 2 | 2 | *John Daniel Hay Lybrand |
| 2 | 4 | 6 | *James Samuel Lybrand |
| 2 | 4 | 6 | *John Myers Lybrand |
| 3 | 8 | 14 | George Samuel Lybrand (Me) |
| 4 | 16 | 30 | Harvey (Harvie) Samuel |
| 5 | 32 | 62 | Lybrand |
| 6 | 64 | 126 | John Samuel Lybrand |
| 7 | 128 | 254 | George Washington Lybrand |
| 8 | 256 | 510 | Wesley Allen Lybrand |
| | | | John N. (Jack) Lybrand, Jr. |

(John, Sr. was the first generation of Lybrand's that was born in South Carolina.)

| 9 | 512 | 1022 | John Lybrand, Sr |

(Christian was born in Germany and came over with his family.)

| 10 | 1024 | 2046 | Christian Lybrand |

(Hendrick Lybrand was born in Germany but immigrated to South Carolina and received the 250-acre land grant that will be talked about in detail.)

| 11 | 2048 | 4094 | Hendrick Lybrand |

(These next five lived in Germany.)

| 12 | 4056 | 8150 | Matthias Leibbrand |
| 13 | 8112 | 16262 | Hans Heinrich Leuprandt |
| 14 | 16224 | 32486 | Hans Michael Leuprandt |
| 15 | 32448 | 64934 | Andreas Leibbrandt |
| 16 | 64896 | 129830 | Wolffgang Leibbrand |

* I have two sons and two grandsons that can carry on the Sam Lybrand line.

This search has proven to me that nothing has changed in human behavior. There were good people and bad people way back then as well as now. The difference between the 1700s and 1800s and now is that there are now no secrets. Modern communication exposes all the bad that we do and the good is buried with our bones. As you will see even the graveyards that some of our ancestors are buried in are covered by the waters of Lake Murray. I have included a detailed account of where John, Sr. and John, Jr. are buried. This graveyard is now covered by Lake Murray. A distant cousin named William B. Rauch provided these details. The Ranch's married into the Lybrand family by marrying one of John Jr's., daughters. Sometimes there is little or nothing left about whom we married and where we are buried much less what we did with our lives. The only thing we can leave behind is what we teach our children and the people that we are exposed to in our lifetime. The most important thing we can leave with our children is our faith in Jesus Christ. If our children are taught the importance of their belief in Jesus Christ then we can rest easy in our eternal home. I like to ask, "In the hereafter where will your children be?" It would be a tragedy if you go to heaven and your children never arrive.

Granddaddy Sam


**Now back to my story:**

To most people the knowledge of where your family comes from is a sense of pride. But let me start off by telling you that after doing some research on my ancestors I have come to realize that after so many generations back we all become kin in some way or the other. If you add up all the people that you are directly kin to as far back as this chapter will reveal, you will find that you have thousands of grandparents that make up your gene pool. But this part of my story just follows the Lybrand line and tells you bits and pieces that I hope make your ancestors come alive and not just be a name with a date of birth and date they died with a dash in between. I hope to make the dash between the names have some meaning and more than just a dash on tombstones out in a lonely graveyard that are seldom visited or thought much about.

I have in my possession a book put together by Doris Lybrand Brittain called **Lybrand Oaks**, copyright in 1982, that has more information than most of us want to know. I talked to her several times when I lived in Irmo, SC. back around 1985. While putting this book together I tried to contact her again and found that she died in her 60s. Her son emailed me and told me of her death. What impressed me about his email was that he had not continued where his mother left off. Therefore, his future generations will only have what his mother put together. I hope this will not happen to my descendants.

I have used several parts of her book in this book. Of course, I will identify the material I use from this book as being from Doris Brittain's book. Her line branches off from a son of John N. (Jack) Lybrand, Jr. Her ancestor was David Deland Lybrand, the brother of Wesley Allen Lybrand. Both were sons of John (Jack) Lybrand. When I finish with Doris Brittain's book, I will give it to my daughter, Amy Lybrand King, for safekeeping.

I also have a book written by Jack Lybrand whose grandfather was George Washington Lybrand. His father and my grandfather, John Samuel Lybrand were brothers. He calls his book From Kleiningersheim to Dutch Fork, Lybrand Descendants of Johann Heinrich Leibbrand and Catherina Weiss. I have used some of his material and have identified the material I used in this book. As in Doris Brittain's book, I will usually refer to his material as being from Jack Lybrand's book.

Let me tell you how I got started on this rabbit trail. Coming up on Edisto Beach we were the only Lybrand's. The only other Lybrand's I really knew anything about were Daddy's people in Charleston. I also remember going to see Granny after we moved to Edisto Beach, SC. Of course, I knew about my life in Aiken before we moved to Edisto and the few trips we took back to Aiken from time to time.

When I got out of college and finished my military service time I ended up in Columbia, SC. Not long after I settled in Columbia, I found the woods to be full of Lybrand's in the Columbia and Lexington area and many of them were black. I asked Daddy about this and he told me that he knew there was a graveyard in New

Holland, SC that went back to 1830 with only Lybrand's buried there. I met a distant cousin named Jack Lybrand, which I have already mentioned, that told me that the Lybrand's had gotten a land grant on the Saluda River above Columbia in 1753 and told me to go down to the Colonial Records on Senate Street in Columbia and they would give me a copy. I went down to the Colonial Records area and found where it had been recorded and wrote down the book and page number. By this time, the old records had been photographed and the records were on tape because they were beginning to fall apart but were still readable. I found the tape with that book on it and went to the page indicated and it was not there. My heart sank. I was rolling up the tape and just happened to notice a Lybrand name four pages back as I rolled up the tape. After looking at it more closely, I found it was the right land grant. I also found the accompanying survey. I took them both to the nice ladies in charge of the records and they made me a copy. Since Daddy was always being "blue blooded" by the people on the island for not being a local and only "beach people", I took the copies I had to an artist and had him draw a scroll around it to make it look official and then had it professionally framed. The first chance I had I took it to Daddy and told him to ask the island people what took them so long to get to South Carolina. His people had been in South Carolina for about 50 years before many of the people's ancestors on Edisto had been on Edisto.

This got me started on what I am going to present in this chapter. Variations of the name go back to the 700s in various spellings and maybe back even further. It is found in Italy and all over Europe and even South Africa. Second Larry recorded that Adam's second cousin was a Lybrand and he warned him to not to eat that apple and to eat an orange instead.

Here are some of the variations I have found: (These are also found in Doris Brittain's book.) Laibbrant - Layprand - Leihbrand - Leiprand - Leiprandt - Lauprandt - Leutprand - Leuttbrand - Leyprand - Luitbrand - Luitprand. From what I can find out, up until fairly recently many people of olden times could not read or write so when their name was recorded the one doing the recording just wrote down what it sounded like to him. I have heard of brothers coming to America through Ellis Island and ending up with two different spellings of their last name. My Amy came across a Lybrand WEB site called Stammbaum der Familien Leibbrandt that had 85 pages of Lybrand's on it with every imaginable spelling of Lybrand. Some of the information I am recording came from this WEB site.

Here is what Doris Brittain had to say about the Lybrand's on pages 25 & 26 of her book.


### Lybrand

"The family name originates in the Old High German personal name Luitprant (Luit = man: Prant = Sword). The literal meaning of the name is "The Most Glorious of the Whole People".

The old form development of the name was: Luitprant, Luitprand, Leyprand, Leyprant, Leyprant, Leiprand, Leipprant. In the seventeenth century the various spelling of the name became Leibbrand and Leibbrandt, although the Steinheim branch of the Bonnigheim Leibbrands retain the old spelling in the form of Leipprand.

A Langobard King was named Luitprant.

In Swabbia during the last of the ninth century a deacon by the name of Luitprant was appointed by King Ludwig as administrator of a chapel in Brenz, and around 1150 a gift to the monastery Allerheiligen in Schafjhausen was given by a man named Luitprant.

The Family name was found earlier only in the Swabain area. Today the name is found in Wurttemberg (especially Leonberg), Weissach, Kleiningersheim, Schwaigern and Stuttgart".

At the beginning of our genealogy (Or this section on the Lybrand's) I have included a Coat of Arms for Leibbrand that I found on the internet. I found this in two different places so I reasoned it must have been a real Coat of Arms. If not, it is nice to know that the family was recognized enough to have a Coat of Arms. But I am certain that our ancestors who came to America care little about a Coat of Arms; instead they were only concerned about staying alive and keeping what they worked for. Maybe if I looked a little further, I could find someone in our past who was a Knight, Earl or Duke who had need for a Coat of Arms.

The following are the Lybrand ancestors I have found and been able to verify. *(There are a few differences in dates from difference sources. I have just chosen the most likely information.)*

In researching every possible avenue about my ancestral line, I came across the following on some large European Lybrand (Leibbrandt) WEB site that told me that Wolffgang Leibbrandt was about as far back as records of the Lybrand's (Leibbrand[t]) go.

"About 1542 in Kirchheim am Neckor a Wolf Leutbrand and in Lau/fen am Nector a Jerg Leyprand were registered. Both are the first ones with the family name Leibbrand whose names were recorded. From here the individual descendants can be traced."

I also found this statement from a Gene Long on the internet which confirmed what I already knew. But it is always nice to confirm from another source what you have already found to be true.

"Johann Hendrick Lybrand ancestors can be found at www.iae.nl, click homepage, click liebbran. Will bring up many pages. Family names goes back to the IJ1h century to Lombard King Liutprand (712-744). Family ancestry goes back to 1542, Wolffgang Liebbrand (Leuttbrand) in Germany."

I brought up the above-mentioned WEB site and it was all in German.

Therefore, I went no further.

In my search it seems that all the Lybrand's with the name Leibbrand(t) came from Wolffgang.

    1. **Wolffgang (Wolfgang) Leibbrandt** - (Lived 72 yrs) - born Vasternorrland, Sweden in 1542-Died 1591 in Kircbheim Neckar, Alemanha, Germany. 1560 married Arnolt.

They had **Andreas Lybrandt** - 1562 - October 24, 1634.

They bad another child **Jerg Leibbrandt**-1567. In my search

Jerg Leibbrandt's name bas often come up. He also began a long line of Lybrand's and is thus a very distant cousin.

They also had **Johannes Leibbrand** who died in 1660.

(In my research I came across Lybrand's that fought on both sides of the Civil war and other Lybrand's that did not fit on my family tree. It stands to reason that these other Lybrand's branched off from distant cousins along the way. At first, I thought the Lybrand's were a small clan but I have found them all over the USA and around the world. Many from the group that came to the Columbia and Lexington, SC area moved west around the time of the Civil War.)

2. **Andreas Leibbrandt** (Lived 72 yrs.)-1562 - October 24, 1634 He lived in Leonberg, Badden (Neckarkreis) Wurttemberg, Germany

   He Married_**Countess Erbach Margaretha**-(Lived 78 yrs.) 1576- October 19, 1634

   They bad **Hans-Michael Ziegler (Ludwig) Leibbrand** - 1595 - February 14, 1669

   They had eight more children.

   **Johannes Pearrer Leibbrand** -1598- March 4, 1659.

   **Anna Leibbrand** - May 24, 1601

   **Margaretha Leibbrand** - February 24, 1602

   **Jeremias Leibbrand**- October 24, 1606

   **Jeremias Leibbrand**-May 12,1608

   **Ursula Leibbrand**-April 6,1610 – married Christina Widmann Sept23,1628

   **Maria Leibbrand** - Died November 11, 1634

(Note: In my research I found some confusion about the

next Lybrand who is a "Hans Lybrand." Back this far there is no telling who was actually kin. Therefore, since I am fairly sure that Wolfgang Lybrand was the first Lybrand actually recorded then I am assuming I have the right "Hans Lybrand."

In addition, as I have gone along in my research, I have recorded all the information I could find. Some information sounds a little strange but with further research one may be able to explain why, like in the above, there were two children with the same name but different birth dates. The way I look at it is that all this information makes these ancestors of ours come alive and not just another Lybrand name with a couple of dates beside their name.)

3. **Hans-Michael Ziegler (Ludwig) Leuprandt (Leibbrand)** - (Lived 85 yrs) - 1595-June 2, 1690 Lived in Kleiningershein, Germany
   He married **Maria** 1599 - February 13, 1677
   They had **Hans Heinrich Leuprandt** born July 8, 1642
   I have found no record of them having any more children.

4. **Hans Heinrich Leuprandt (Leibbrand)** - (Lived 76 yrs.) -July 8, 1642 - Sept. 1, 1718 also lived in Kleiningersheim, Germany
   He married **Sofie Baerkler-** (Lived 47 yrs.) 1640-1687
   And Marie Agnes - (Lived 52 yrs.) 1665 -Died 1717
   He and Sofie had Mattias Leibbrand born 1670 They had two other children not in our line.
   **Johann Heinrich Leibbrand**-January 14,1664-March 31, 1732
   **Hansierg Ambrosius Leibbrand** - 1675 = Married Barbara Faber

<u>5</u>. **Matthias Leibbrandt** born 1670 - Lived in Kleiningsheim, Germany

He married Margaretha -1672-Death unknown

> They had **Johann Heinrich Leibbrand** -1695 They had three other children not in our line.
>
> **Anna Maria Leibbrand** - January 1705 - Married Andreas Valet
>
> **Andrew Friedrich Leibbrand** - November 30. 1715, married Susanna Ayenpres.
>
> **Johann Jacob Leibbrand** - January 28, 1717, married Maria Veronica

6. **Johann Heinrich Leibbrand** - (Lived 78 yrs) -1695 - 1773 born in Liver Kleiningersheim, Germany

> He married **Catharine Weiss** - (Lived 54 yrs.) Born 1708 - 1762 - (Daughter of **Jacob Weiss**) on November 14, 1724 in Germany. They had **Johann Jacob Leibbrand** - March 22, 1726 who was born in Germany and died in Germany December 7, 1795
>
> He married **Maria Margaretha Feydinger** - April 18, 1752
>
> As far as I can determine Johann Jacob Leibbrand and his wife did not come to Charles Town with his father or ever after.
>
> Hendrick came to Charles Town and settled in the upcountry of SC.
>
> **Johann Christian Leibbrand** - October 8, 1728 who was born in Germany.
>
> **Maria Catharina Leibbrand** - August 20, 1731 who was born in Germany
>
> **Simeon Leibbrand** and **Ambrosius Leibbrand** twins born July 29, 1734 in Germany
>
> **Margaretha Barbara Leibbrand** - May 26, 1737 who was born in Germany.

In December of 1752, after his oldest son was married and settled, Johann Heinrich Leibbrand traveled up the Rhine River to the Port of Rotterdam, Holland, paid for himself and the members of his family that included his wife, Christian, Simon and Maria on the ship "Elizabeth" (Ship's Captain William McCall) bound for the port of Charles Town, South Carolina in December 1752. They arrived February of 1753. He changed his name to **Johann Hendrick Lybrand** and applied for a land grant. I'll give you more details further on in this Chapter.

7.    **Johann Christian Leibbrand (Lybrand)** - Born October 8, 1728 in Germany- Died in Lexington County, SC in the 1800s-I have found no record of who he married

    They had **John Lybrand, Sr.** 1760 August 10, 1820 They had three other children.

    **Christopher Lybrand** - 1756 - married Barbara

    **Joseph Lybrand** - 1762 -married Margaret Magdalene Wessinger in 1789 in Lexington, SC

    **Henry Lybrand** 1770 - 1811 - married Mary Barbara Ballentine

8.  **John Lybrand, Sr.** (Lived 60 yrs.) - 1760 - August 10, 1820 - One reference says he was born in North Carolina

    He married **Mary (Anna Nancy) Benay (Anna Senior)-** (Lived 72 yrs.) 1765 - 1837

    They had **John N. (Jack) Lybrand, Jr.** - May 1, 1791 - Married Mary Magdalene Wessinger

    They had five more children.

    One was **Henry Lybrand** - Born 1783 who gave the land for St. James Lybrand Lutheran Church - He married Nancy Ballentine

Joseph Lybrand -1785 - Sept 8, 1876
**William Lybrand** - 1787 - Married Barbara Sease
**Annie Lybrand** - 1795 - Married Elijah Hendrix
**Isaac Lybrand** - 1796 - Died 1861 in Arkansas - Married Anna Barbara Wessinger

9. **John N. (Jack) Lybrand, Jr.** - (Lived 70 yrs.) May 1, 1791 - 1861

> He married <u>Sarah Elizabeth Fulmer</u> on February 18, 1813 Elizabeth was born May 6, 1795 - March 1865 (Lived 69 yrs.)
>
> > They had **Wesley Allen Lybrand** - January 9, 1823 - April 11, 1908
> >
> > > *Wesley Allen Lybrand lost his arm in the battle of Atlanta during the Civil War Wesley moved to New Holland in 1850. John Jr. and Sarah had 9 other children
> > >
> > > **Martha Rutha Lybrand** - September 9, 1814 - Aug. 29 1912 - She married Emmanual Derrick

**David Delano Lybrand** - Oct.24, 1817 -Dec. 1888 - buried Marvin Chapel Cemetery, Van Zandt County, Texas.
Dec. 6, 1838 married <u>Anna Elizabeth Stingley.</u>
Moved to Alabama and on to Attalla County, Miss. in 1843 & to Smith County, Texas in 1850-This is the ancestor of Doris Brittain who wrote the book **Lybrand Oaks.**
His first wife died and he married **<u>Mary Elizabeth Jefferies.</u>**

**John Lybrand, IV** - 1815

***Joshua Levi Lybrand** - July 20, 1820 - Died Feb. 23, 1862 in the Civil War.
Private Joshua Levi Lybrand enlisted in Company I, 15th Regiment of SC in the infantry on December 10,

1861. His career in the service ended February 23, 1862 at Camp Elliot on the coast near Savannah, Georgia. Some say that he died of some disease like his brother John Noah did of Typhoid Dysentery. Married **Mary Eve Frazier.**
Joshua and Mary moved to Miss. and moved back to Chapin, SC when his father became blind and ill.

**Mary Ann Elizabeth Lybrand** - July 20, 1825 - 1919 - She married Hillard Rauch - This is the ancestor of the William B. Rauch who provided the information on the original Jack Lybrand property.

**Lucinda Caroline Lybrand** - February 27, 1828 - July 27, 1890 - she married Elias Cohen Frick

*****Louisa Selinda Lybrand** - December 9, 1830 - March 5, 1933
She married Henry Matthias Wessinger- he died June 26, 1862 in the battle of Hilton Head during Civil War

*****Chaney Francis Lybrand** -August 17, 1833 -1930 - she married Jessie Ballentine about 1840.
Married Jacob Francis Koon 1857- He died in 1871 from wounds received during Civil War
Married William Franklin Koon, brother of Jacob Koon.

*****John Noah Lybrand** - September 20, 1836 - June 1, 1862 - died in Civil War at the age of 26.
John Noah Lybrand enlisted for the duration of the Civil War in Dutch Fork, SC. Private Lybrand was promoted from rank to second lieutenant December 11, 1861. He died of typhoid dysentery the first day of June, 1962 at Hardeeville, SC.

**Jacob J. Lybrand** -Sept. 20, 1839 - Death unk. - married Sallie Harlen - Moved to Texas and died in Texas

* **Note:** Civil War results of John N. (Jack)
Lybrand's family are as follows:

- Wesley Allen Lybrand lost his arm in the battle of Atlanta.
- Joshua Levi Lybrand died.
- Louisa Celinda Lybrand's husband Henry Matthias Wessinger died in the Battle of Hilton Head.
- Chancy Francis Lybrand's second husband Jacob Koon died as a result of wounds received during the Civil War.
- John Noah Lybrand died.

Therefore, in this family two sons died, two sons-in-law died and one son was badly wounded. Five out of ten children were affected. Happily, our ancestor, George Washington Lybrand, Wesley Allen's son, was born in 1848 which would have made him around 12 or 13 years old at the time of the Civil War and was too young to serve in the war.

**Note:** In my research I found that 57 Lybrand's served in the Union and Confederate armies. I found 33 Lybrand's that served on the Confederate side and 14 on the Union side. There may be more Lybrand's that served but this is what I found. I was not able to confirm that we were kin to all those that served in this awful war.

10. **Wesley Allen Lybrand** - (Lived 85 yrs.) January 9, 1823-April 11, 1908

He was born in the Chapin area and died in the New Holland, SC area.

He married **Sarah Elizabeth (Sallie) Derrick**- (Lived 81 yrs.) February 11, 1826 - March 25, 1907

They were married January 18,1844

They had **(G.W.) George Washington Lybrand** - Nov. 19, 1848 - June 5, 1935 - My father told me that George Washington Lybrand was called G.W. and it was not until later in life that he found out his full name.

Wesley Allen Lybrand lost his arm in the Battle for Atlanta During the Civil War.

They had 13 more children; only 10 lived to adulthood. (They moved to the New Holland area in 1850.)

**David Calhoun Lybrand** - Sept. 29, 1846 - Nov. 9, 1846

**Joseph Andrew Lybrand** - July 18, 1853 - July 6, 1862

**John William Lybrand** -Dec. 2, 1851 - Dec. 3, 1919 - married Anne Donie Jackson

**Henry Patrick Lybrand** - Jan. 18,1855 - Oct 30, 1856

**Frances Permelia Lybrand** - 1856- July 11, 1943 - Married Leroy F. Boatwright

**Noah Webster Lybrand**-Feb. 23, 1859-July28, 1882- Married Minnie Wells

**Jacob Wesley Lybrand** - December 18, 1861 - Nov. 3, 1923

**Amanda Lybrand** (I found no information on her.)

**Amelia Lybrand** married John Boatright

**Sarah Alice Lybrand** - February 3, 1864 - 1945 - Married Wilson Uriah Wessinger

**Louisa Joanner Lybrand** - January 3, 1866 - Dec. 16, 1938 married Paul Swartz

**Manervia C. Lybrand** - April 1, 1868 - July 24, 1930

married Furman Huckabee

**Walter Franklin Lybrand**-November 3, 1870-
Dec.13, 1929- Married Lula Shealy and
Margaret Baughman Coleman (Note: most of
the above information came from Jack
Lybrand's book.)


11. **George Washington Lybrand**- (Lived 86 yrs.)
November 19, 1848 - June 5, 1935.
He married **Sara Jane Jackson** -(Lived 69 yrs.)
July 21, 1856 -Nov. 24,1925
They had **John Samuel Lybrand**-May 3,
1872-Nov.28, 1924
They had 9 more children.
My daddy, Harvie Lybrand, told me he had 60
first cousins; many are listed in the write ups
below.

(Under George Washington Lybrand I am putting information that I got from LeMyra Tyler Young. She currently lives in Wagener where several of my ancestors lived. She is the great-granddaughter of George Washington Lybrand and Sara Jane Jackson. She currently writes for the **Wagener Monthly** and has been a great help in putting together my Lybrand story. The information she furnished is in italics under each child of George Washington. I have copied her information on George Washington's children just as she wrote it so I would not miss the flavor of her writing. This is a warning, "Be nice to your relatives." She only gave me limited information on John Samuel and Mamie because she assumed, I already had information on them. As I recorded the information LeMyra gave me I recognized many of the names because from time to time Daddy mentioned them. Comments made by me about some of the people LeMyra talked about are enclosed in brackets [----]. Most of the dates of Wesley Allen and George Washington

came from Jack Lybrand. I am assuming they are right.
Their other 9 children were:

**H.B Lybrand** June 24, 1874 - June 24, 1874 - Died as an Infant

**J.G. Lybrand** - October 19, 1875 - May 28, 1887

**George Tillman Lybrand** -October 28, 1878 -Sept. 11, 1936 - Married Myrtis Lillian Shull

**George** married Myrtis Shull: he was a/armer and lived in New Holland, SC. Aunt Myrtis ran a boarding house in Wagener so that she could send her children to college. All of her children attended business school or college. Their children: Grady Omar married Estelle when they were both in their 40's. They lived in Wagener. She taught school and Grady entertained most everyone with his jokes and sold insurance on the side. <u>Nell</u> married Frank Briggs. They too were older when they married, Nell was some sort of secretary in Columbia when she met Frank. However, they made their home in Wagener. He owned the Ford Dealership in Wagener: I remember well when he owned one of the first Lincoln Continentals. It seemed as big as a box car and was a convertible with white leather upholstery; the back doors opened to the left Nell did not work after she married Frank. They built a showplace home for Wagener standards. Frank sold the Ford dealership, and retired so to speak. He did open the first laundromat in Wagener, and it is still in operation today. **Jimmie** "Jim" married Bill Mixon. She taught school for a while and Bill was a salesman. Both of them were pillars of Wagener United Methodist Church. Bill left a multimillion-dollar estate including several large tracts of land. **Mertie Leo "Byrd"** married Marshall Voight I know little of them since they did not live in Wagener. **Hope** taught school until she married Wayne Williamson, a general practitioner. He had his office in Wagener, and they built another showplace home near Frank and Nell. Hope had two sons; they are the only grandchildren of Uncle George and Aunt Myrtis. Hope died in her early 40's of a self-inflicted gunshot wound.

**Carrie Cornelia Lybrand** - June 19, 1883 - Nov. 30, 1970, Married Jeter Mathis Ready

Corrie (Pronounced Carrie) married Jeter Ready. They lived between New Holland and Oak Grove. He was an only child and apparently came from a family of means. He finished Clemson but never worked, He drove His Ford to Aiken every day and sat around the court house talking with the other men sitting around the court house. [Note: the court house was a couple of blocks from where we lived in Aiken on the same side of the street.] Mama remembers that Uncle Jeter wore a ten-gallon hat and when he was at home sat on the front porch with his feet propped up. Their children: Annie married Euse Hutto; he was a farmer and a logger. Annie taught school for a while; Annie and Euse had 8 children. Sally was married twice; her last husband was an American Indian with the last name of Cash. Sally had 2 sons by her first husband Thomas Craig. She owned Cash's Grocery in Aiken. Derotha "D.O." was married twice and had one daughter. Patrick Henry "Pat" married Imogene Hall and had two children. Johnnie never married. Eugene Buckingham "Punk" married Jenny and had one son. Punk worked for Aiken Rural Electric. James never married and lacked one semester from graduating from Furman University. He was expelled for making liquor in his room. Faye married Grady Smith and had one daughter.

**Allen Bowman Lybrand** - January 12, 1885 - June 6, 1969 - Married Lennie Ethel Hutto and Cora Belle Toole

Allen first married Lennie Hutto. He was a farmer. Their children: **Gussie** married G.L Cook; they had two children. G.L. killed Gussie; and then killed himself. **Anita** married A.W. Stoudemire and had three children. After Lennie died, Uncle Allen married Cora Toole. She was 20 years younger. Their children: Al Dessie married Joyce Hair and had two children. Al had a beautiful voice. He sang in the church choir and for funerals and weddings. [Note: I knew Al while living in Columbia and knew of his singing talent.] **James** "Jim" married Catjerin Jones; they had one child. They were married for a very short time. He then married Linda Widerner; they had two children. He has been married to Pam Cooper for close to 30 years. [Jim is a very good man; he just made some unlucky choices in women.] Jim has worked at various jobs dealing with the public. He has retired several times but still works part time in Tyler Brothers in Wagener. **Vicki Jane** died at 4 years of age.

**Cora Lee Lybrand**-March 7,1887 -May 16,1938- Married Michael Albert Smith

**Cora** married Mike Smith. He was from Batesburg; however, they lived in Wiliston; Uncle Mike farmed. Their children: Herbert married Elizabeth McKeon; they had one child. **Lybrand** [Called Mike Smith of Edisto Island.) married Jean Wilkinson [of Edisto Island.]; they had three children. Daniel died at age 22.) (Note: Jann Poston, Jean Wilkinson Smith's daughter currently lives close to me on Edisto Island. When I was coming up, I stayed with the Smiths who lived on Frampton Creek while my parents left the Island. I also went to school with Jann. Mike Smith helped build the improved paved road on Edisto in the late 1930s.

**Fred Clay Lybrand** - April 15, 1890 - Jan, 3, 1954, married Leile Blanche Cafer

**Fred*** married Leila Cofer (my grandparents) They lived in New Holland and in Wagener. Pa Fred was a farmer and a carpenter. Their children: <u>Cofer</u> married Edith Smith and had no children. **Virginia** died at 20 months during the great flu epidemic of 1918. **Marion** married Adine Johnson and had two girls. [Earlier I mentioned the 90+ year old that wrote me about my Daddy teaching him in the New Holland Grammar School in 5th grade and him being the only one that made a 100 on a math test, well this is the one that wrote me.] **Norman** married Joyce Beam and had ten (yes, ten) children. Joyce was from Pa., and they lived there all their married life. Uncle Norman's children and grandchildren are the only Lybrand's in their area. **Frances** married C.E. "Gene" Tyler, Jr. and has one daughter Le Myra [The one that wrote all this] and one son Charles E Taylor, IIL Gene Tyler was 3rd generation in grocery stores: Mama began full time work in the store when my younger brother Charlie started school. Daddy closed the store in 2001. The business had been in operation for 97 years. My brother Charlie and my son Tyler were 4'h and 5t1, generations working in the business when it closed. My brother has a Master's in Business and Masters in Education; he is employed with Aiken County School District and is presently at the district office as a Title One coordinator. My son has an associate degree in Electronic Engineering and one in Computer Engineering and is employed with Simples Grinell. They were both fortunate in that they were able to be employed just after Daddy closed the Store. <u>Jack</u> married Melba Baughman and has one son. [Jack Lybrand is the one I met in Columbia, SC in the 1980s and got me started on finding out all I could about the Lybrand's.] Jack was career Air force, and upon retirement taught vocational education courses at the high school level (and makes money on the side selling his genealogy info). **Bobby** is married to Mary Terry and has two daughters. [I talked to Bobby at the suggestion of my son Jimmy Lybrand who lives in Pelion, SC. He is the one that put me in touch with his sister Frances. This search has led me from one person to another person to gather all this information recorded in this book.] Bobby was also career Air force and taught vocational education courses at Aiken High School. Bobby's wife Mary is my husband's aunt /Garry's mother's sister]. Mary and Garry are both from, Tulsa, OK. /Bobby and Mary live at Wagener's only gated community, Lake Edisto.]

*All of Fred and Leila's children and Jim Lybrand are extremely talented in creative design, carpentry, wood craft, fuel engines, electricity, etc. Frances has made over 50 quilts, has always made all of her own clothes and mine when I was growing up; she has a creative skill that is hard to explain. My brother Charlie falls into this category too. I got left out; my skill is talking. I mention the above because I truly feel that their creativeness is from the Lybrand's.

**Bessie Lou Lybrand** - August 14, 1891 - April 11, 1975
Married Dr. John Holmam Brodie, MD

**Bessie** married Dr. J.H. Brodie, the beloved Wagener physician. Aunt Bessie kept the nursery at Wagener United Methodist Church for over 50 years. The nursery room was just a door away from the sanctuary at the time of her death. I remember at her funeral as the preacher was telling of Aunt Bessie's faithfulness, the nursery room creaked and opened slowly as if on cue. I was one of those babies born at home. When Mama went into labor, Daddy went for Dr. Brodie; he told Daddy to get Josephine, the black midwife, and that he would come to see about Mama after he saw about a drunk on the other side of the river. Well, Josephine delivered me: Dr. Brodie got there in time to cut the cord. Josephine always called me one of her white babies. Their children: **George** married Grace Blakeney and had three children. George was County Agent for Allendale County, and Grace was a school principal. **Maxine** never married; she worked for DSS. Maxine and I became close when we were working together on the joint bereavement dinner committee of the Baptist and Methodist Churches. She was a terrific person and a good sport. She died of lung cancer.

**Eula Jane Lybrand**-August 12,1893-Nov.23, 1979- Married George McDonald (Donley) Rish

**Eula Jane "Nig"** married George "Donley" Rish. Aunt Nig was always happy. She played the piano and organ for many years at Wagener United Methodist Church. Their children: **Donnie Ray** married Margaret Howell and had no children. **Betty** married Barney Rogers and has two children.

The next several pages are pictures I have gotten from several sources.

These are pictures of two of George Washington's sons. **Fred Clay Lybrand** on the left. Jack Lybrand, his son, furnished the picture. **Allen Bowman Lybrand** & **Cora Toole Lybrand** below. Jimmy Lybrand, their son, furnished the picture.

The following has to be one of favorite pictures. I received two copies of this picture after many tries to get a copy. LeMyra Young and Jack Lybrand each furnished me a copy. This picture was taken in 1904. I have two names for this baseball team: **Sand Dam Baseball Team** & **Seivern Baseball Team**. I understand that Sammy Lybrand was the team manager. (My Daddy's mailing address in the early 1900s was Seivern, SC.)
Standing is *John Samuel (Sammy) Lybrand, my grandfather
On the front row is: Kence Hutto, *Fred Lybrand-George Washington's son Ode Huto, Chester Brogdin *George Lybrand-George Washington's son
On the second row is: Euse Hutto *Allen Lybrand - George Washington's Son, Milledge Shull, E.H. "Bub" and Gunter Newt Lucas
* Brothers: Sammy, Fred, George, and Allen.

This is also one of my favorite pictures. It was also furnished by LeMyra Young. It is a picture of ladies sitting around smoking pipes. I find it interesting to find old pictures with the generations mixing.

On the front row: Jane Jackson Lybrand, George Washington's Wife. Permelia Lybrand Boatwright, George Washington's Sister, and Lucy Ann Gunter Shull.

On the Second row: Alice Lybrand Wessinger, George Washington's sister. Edna Fallow Shull, Geneva Shull Gunter, Sally H. Kirkland, and Martha Kenny

The small child in front of Jane Jackson Lybrand is "Byrd" Lybrand, daughter of George and granddaughter of Jane and George Washington.

This picture was taken in about 1995. It was furnished by Jimmy Lybrand. It was a gathering of George Washington's grandchildren. Only a few are still alive at the time of the writing of this book. My brother David Lybrand took my father (in the red sweater) to this gathering.

From left to right: Bobby Lybrand, Fred's son
    Cofer Lybrand, Fred's son
    Francis Lybrand Tyler, Fred's son
    George Marion Lybrand, Fred's son
    Harvie Samuel Lybrand, Sammy's son
    Herbert Smith, Cora Lybrand Smith's son
    Jimmy Lybrand Mixon, George Lybrand's daughter
    Jack Lybrand, Fred's son
    Maxine Brodie, Bessie Lybrand Brodie's Daughter
    George Rish, Nig Lybrand Rish's son
    Nita Lybrand Stoudermire, Allen Lybrand's Daughter
    George Albert Brodie, Bessie Lybrand Brodie's son
    Al D. Lybrand, Allen Lybrand's son
    Jimmy Lybrand, Allen Lybrand's son

When you bear about the old New Holland school and that George Washington raised large horses, they come alive when you see a picture of them. This picture is of George Washington and his wife Jane in a buggy in front of the New Holland school where my father taught. This picture was given to me by LeMyra Young.

This is a picture of the New Holland Methodist Church that George Washington Lybrand gave the land and lumber to build. Jimmy Lybrand sent me this picture. As I have stated before it pleases me to know that the Lybrand clan has been involved in helping build the St. James (Lybrand) Lutheran Church, the Macedonia Lutheran Church, the New Holland Methodist Church and the St. Andrews Presbyterian.

I am not sure how he fits into the Lybrand clan but the Lybrand's have raised at least one preacher. Here is information I got from two sources. I am rally not sure where the first one came from. The second one came from the St. Peters Lutheran Church WEB site.

Pastor Eli Lot Lybrand, born in 1852, was pastor of the Mount Tabor Lutheran Church, in the Greater Columbia, SC area from 1895 to 1919. He also served time in the State Legislature and was trained in medicine as well as theology. The small picture at the right is of his family. All I can find out about him is that he was a well-loved man of God.

I also came across Rev. E.L Lybrand who served as an interim Pastor for the St. Peters Lutheran Church in Chapin, SC during the time the older Lybrand's lived in this area. I think this is the same person. I could not verify this or figure out how they were tied to our Lybrand clan.

12. **John Samuel Lybrand** - (Lived 52 yrs) - May 3, 1872 - November 28, 1924

> He married **Mamie Louise Clayton** - (Lived 94 yrs.)-July 7, 1878 - March 16, 1973
>
>> They had **Harvie Samuel Lybrand** - August 2, 1904 November 25, 1997
>>
>> They also had 4 other children.
>>
>> **Essie Lybrand** - September 30, 1900 - December 5, 1900 - Died as an infant.
>>
>> **Thelma Jane Lybrand** - September 26, 1901 - May 5, 1927 - Married Fed Quitman Hydrick. Died in childbirth with 5th child. The child also died.
>>
>> **Harvie (Harvey) Samuel Lybrand**-Aug 2, 1904-Nov.2, 1997 - Married Jennie Brown Owens and had three children - after my mother died, he married Evelyn Margaret McPherson around 1989 or a couple years after my mother died.
>>
>> **Charlie Clayton (Jack) Lybrand** - Feb. 24,1908 - Feb 27, 1983 - Married Erna Gertrude Butler
>>
>> **Susie (Sue) Lybrand** -Nov. 3,1910- Oct. 1986 - Married Jack William Smithson and Charlie Robert Parker

Here is a letter that my grandmother Mamie received from her older sister in 1933. I have recorded the content and a copy of the envelope. Note that the envelope's address has no street address, no ZIP code and the stamp was only three cents.

*"January 3, 1933, Greenville, SC My dear Mamie,*

*I received your sweet card a few days ago. Was glad to get. How are you all and the rest of our folks getting along, I never do hear from any of them.*

*We have had a lot of rain here. And it is faire now but it is freezing cold I nearly freeze here ever winter. We had a very pleasant xmas. Estelle and her family took dinner with me. I gave them a nice turkey dinner. She has two smart children. They are a lot of pleasure to me. Myrtle is working for the same people she has been there 10 years. My children are a lot of pleasure to me in my old age.*

*Where is Holley living now and also Harvey teaching school this winter? Mamie I would like to see you. I think of you and Holly how you looked when you both were little children.*

*My health isn't very good. I manage to keep up all the time. I want you to write back to me and tell me about ever body. Myrtis sends her love to you. You must excuse bad writing and spelling.*

*With much love to you all. Your sister Maggie Plunkett"*

The address on the back of the envelope is:

Mrs. N.E. Plunkett
306 Arlington Ave.
Greenville, SC

This is the envelope it came in. Note that the end is torn off to get into the letter. I can still see my father sitting down with a bunch of letters and tearing off the end just as this envelope is torn. I do the same when I open a letter. I guess ways of doing thing and habits are really passed down from one generation to another without anyone really taking notice. I never gave it much thought until I saw this old letter and the way it was opened.

A couple of more pictures of Granny

This next picture was taken at our house on Edisto Beach, SC of Granny Lybrand and some of the Harvie and Jennie Lybrand's family, taken in the early 1970s. This was a few years before Granny died. She was in her 90s when this was taken. Everyone except Josephine, Lizette and Ida have Granny's blood flowing in their veins.

**Back row:**
> Josephine, Tommy's wife,
> Debra, Josephine's daughter
> Me.
> David, my brother
> Lisette, David's first wife

**2nd Row:**
> Jenny, Josephine's daughter
> Amy, my daughter
> Dickie, Josephine's son
> Jimmy, my son
> Ida, my first wife

**3rd Row:**
> Edith, Josephine's daughter
> Granny
> John, my son

**Seated in front of Edith:**
> Kim, David's daughter

13. **Harvie Samuel Lybrand** (Lived 93 yrs.) August 2, 1904-
November 25, 1997

He married **Jennie Brown Owens**_(Lived 77
yrs.) - March 4, 1910 - June 6, 1987
They had **George Samuel {Sam) Lybrand** (Me)
- April 3, 1937 - Present
They had 2 other children.
**Thomas Harvie Lybrand**  (Lived 38 yrs.)-
April 5, 1933 -January 18, 1972- Married
Josephine Ethel LaRoche
**David Ladson Lybrand** - June 23, 1941 -
Present - Married Lisette Ann Tunnel and
Doris Scoville

14. **George Samuel Lybrand** - April 3, 1937 to present (2012)
I married **Ida Margaret Myers** September 19,
1936 - died March, 2000

We were married December 23, 1959-After
Ida died, I married Joyce Hills Abrams,
November 25, 2000.

Ida and I had **James Samuel Lybrand** -
October 11, 1960 -- Present - Jim's son
Samuel Dupree Lybrand is the 16th
Lybrand that can carry on the Sam
Lybrand clan to the 17th generation.
We had 2 other children
**Amy Margaret Lybrand** - January 22, 1963
- Present - She married Matthew
Chamberlain King
**John Myers Lybrand** - August 21, 1965 -
Present - He Married Elizabeth (Liz)
Ann Hay - Their son John Daniel Hay
Lybrand is also the 16th Lybrand that can
carry on the Sam Lybrand clan to the 1ih
generation.

15. **James Samuel Lybrand** - October 11, 1960 - Present 2012
He married **Melinda Jozette Starnes** July 21,
1958- Present
They have 2 children
**Samuel Dupree Lybrand** December 20, 1986 -
Present **Laken Jozette Lybrand** - December 20, 1989
- Present


15. **Amy Margaret Lybrand King** - January 22, 1963 - Present
She married **Matthew Chamberlain King.**
The have 3 children
**Anne Harley King** -May 4, 1993 - Present
**James Oliver King**- June 17, 1995 - Present
**Robert David King** - April 30, 2004 - Present


15. **John Myers Lybrand** - August 21, 1965 - Present - He
married **Elizabeth (Liz) Ann Hay.**
They have 2 Children
**John Daniel Hay Lybrand** - June 7, 1998 - Present
**Sarah Elizabeth Lybrand** - May 25, 2002 - Present

16. **Samuel Dupree Lybrand** - Dec. 20, 1986 - *These two can carry
on to*
16. **John Daniel Hay Lybrand** - June 7, 1998 *the 17ᵗʰ generation.*


As of 2012 there has been a male Lybrand for approximately 470 years through 16 generations.

In doing my research of the Lybrand name I have found that from the two sons of Hendrick Lybrand the woods have become full of Lybrand's not only in South Carolina but in many other states. After the Civil War and maybe before that many of the Lybrand clan started moving west. I have found the Lybrand name all over the United States, particularly in the lower states. There were several other Lybrand's that moved to the United States with such names as Liebbrandt and a few other variations but most of those I have found are descendants of Hendrick Lybrand, particularly in South Carolina.

To give a real sense of what our people have meant to the northwest part of the Greater Columbia, SC area, now commonly known as the "Dutch Fork" area, I found the following two articles in Jack Lybrand's paper on the Lybrand's. This is the area that the first Lybrand received his land grant. Here is how it is presented. Anyone with the Lybrand name or another German name would stand proud after reading these articles preserved by Jack Lybrand.

*"The following two articles, The "Dutch Fork" is German Fork, and "Dutch Fork" Germans Remember, were written by N. Harrison Jenkins and appeared in the State paper the year that South Carolina was celebrating its 30flh birthday.*

### THE "DUTCH FORK" IS GERMAN FORK
Achtung:

*May nothing less than continuous prosperity shower bountiful blessings upon the merchants of Greater Columbia's Dutch Square mall. May their cash registers ever tinkle a merry tone; may they thrive and flourish like the tulips of the Netherlands, but*

*The symbol that has been chosen is that of the Netherlands, of Holland- and these Dutch have a lot to do with windmills (the symbol) but contributed absolutely nothing to the naming of the place where Dutch Square is, the "Dutch Fork" of South Carolina.*

*It's German .. Has been .. Always.*

*THUS, the symbol of the windmill is indeed the prerogative of the merchant, but no Carolinian should be misled into thinking that Hollanders had anything to do with the Dutch Fork. German Protestants gave the area its name.*

*Dutch (From "Deutach" or "Deutachland") means German. In short, the "Dutch Fork" of South Carolina is "German Fork" and, emphatically, not "Holland Fork".*

*English-speaking people were using the word "Dutch" to refer to the Germans, and all things German, long before the American colonies were founded. Use of "Dutch" to mean German extends back into the 14th and J5t1, centuries and was, quite naturally, used by the colonists in the North and South.*

*For example, "Pennsylvania Dutch" is one of the very few genuine American dialects, in the narrowest sense of the term. "Pennsylvania Dutch" is that English spoken by Germans who came to the Quaker State. In 1753, 36 years before the great influx of Germans to Pennsylvania, Benjamin Franklin wrote: "Advertisements, intended to be general, are now printed in Dutch (i.e., German) and English."*

*THE GERMANS who came to South Carolina entered through Savannah or Charleston and later some others drifted down from Pennsylvania. (The Salzburgers who came through Savannah, were remnants of the 30,000 Austrian Protestants who refused to conform to Roman Catholicism and were given protection of a German king.)*

*The Germans who migrated from the Low country to Saxe-Gotha (later Lexington County), into the area quickly became farmers, who cultivated the not-so- desirable soil of the area with remarkable success. They were also present in the interior parts of the province of South Carolina as a buffer between the predominantly English colony on the coast and the Indians.*

*The Germans survived their share of suffering. One early chronicler wrote, "Wheat is cultivated with much success, by the German Protestants, who are settled on the interior parts of the province; they would have been able to supply the province with all the flour we consume, by this time, had they not been interrupted by the Cherokee War.*

*"These industrious people distill a palatable brandy from peaches, which they have in great plenty; likewise, from potatoes, Indian corn and rye."*

*These sturdy German tilled their farms, built their churches, lived to themselves and built-by blood, sweat and tears-the Dutch Fork.*

*By the mid-19th century, residents of Columbia even referred to the area so widely known) as simply "The Fork." Everyone knew it was German. A contemporary noted that one of these industrious Germanic housekeepers still "spoke quiet Dutchy." "The people had all the characteristics and peculiarities of their forefathers in*

*Germany; honesty, industry, economy, submission to their rules in Church and State... The people worked hard and lived cheaply, buying nothing but absolute necessities, except whiskey and tobacco for the men and, perhaps, ribbons and calico for the women."*

*INDEED, these characteristics prevail even today. Try driving a bargain with a Dutch Fork (German) descendant today. He's a tough bargainer, down to the last penny.*

*Now, there's a personal interest in the Dutch Fork. During a recent week's stay on Lake Murray, I toted my wife (born Ruth Bundrick) and our children (Carolyn Anne and Olin Bundrick) around the Dutch Fork graveyards to inspect the burial spots of their forebears.*

*Some we found at the "butter-and-eggs" church of Mt. Tabor at Little Mountain. There rest the children's great grandparents, Mr. and Mrs. Charlie Bundrick; their great-great grandparents on the Shealy side; and their great-great- great grandfather, Jacob Shealy.*

*We also drove over to aging but still beautiful Bethlehem church near Pomaria, where the Bundricks were laid to rest. We have yet to trace the Bowers side of the children's maternal forebears--but the genealogists of Chapin have promised help.*

*A windmill for Dutch Square? The merchants may have chosen. But it's still right in the middle of the Dutch (German) Fork and Carolinians should be aware that Holland contributed nothing to the history of the area, windmill or not windmill.*

*In a way, you see, it's quite like someone deciding that - after all - Charleston was really named after some French king named Charles. Then historic Charles Town could adopt the fleur-de-lis as its symbol."*

### "Dutch Fork" Germans Remember

*In this tricentennial year of South Carolina's nativity, the man of historical consciousness might wonder if Carolinians have disremembered their past. Wonder little, friend.*

*Last week I questioned whether a sense of history pervaded our thought, because the proprietors of Dutch Square Mall had adapted the windmill as the symbol of their covered center of shops, dropped right in the middle of the "Dutch Fork." The Dutch Fork was named/or Germans; not Hollanders. That, I thought, everyone knew.*

*Wouldn't it have been the height of impropriety, as Carolina lit 300 candles on its birthday cake, to have invited down the Netherlands ambassador and some of the Netherlands' royalty to honor the windmill? That, indeed, would have been grievous injury to the thousands of descendants of the sturdy Germans who cut their homes and churches and/arms out of the German Fork wilderness!*

*Fortunately, literally scores of the direct lineal children of the 1730-1769 settlers of the German fork areas in Richland, Lexington, Newberry and Saluda counties responded to the column. My gratitude and thanks to their manifold kindness. To mention them all would be to roll call the names of their forebears. A partial listing includes: Bowers, Bundrick, Caughman, Cousins, Counts, Derrick, Drafts, Fulmer, Geiger, Harmon, Havird, Houseal, Keisler, Kinard, Koon, Lindler, Lybrand, Mets (and all its variants), Quattlebaum, Rawl, Roof, Sease, Shealy, Sox, Varn, Wessinger, Wingard, Wise, Younginer, and Zeigler.*

*These families-and many more-remember well their lineage. Happily, they have for the honest Carolina historians know: that the Germans (particularly those from the Palatine) are the Forgotten Men among the colonists. "Numerically the Germans were the third largest European nationality to settle in South Carolina, the largest being the English and the second the Scotch -Irish."*

*Our historians have concentrated on the Charleston area, the Piedmont and the Pee Dee - with latter day attention concentrated on our urbanizing area. Yet, quietly and unobtrusively, the sturdy "Dutchman" (the German) of the Fork have played an important part in our state's history. They have been largely ignored, as have their manifold contribution in the colonial, Revolutionary, Civil War, post-helium and modern periods.*

*There is a short history of their deeds and their valor available, free. It was written by my one-time colleague and all-time friend Professor Daniel W. Hollis of the University of South Carolina. It's entitled "A History of*

*St. Andrews and The Dutch Fork" and can be obtained gratis at any office of Home Federal Saving & Loan Association, which commissioned the chronicle.*

*In the concentrated history, Dr. Hollis says, "The fact that the South Carolina "Dutch" have tended to forego politics may be partially responsible for the neglect they have received from Palmetto writers."*

*THAT IS as he acknowledges, part-but only part-of the reason. The Dutch Fork Germans came to the state with noble dreams, were given frontier earth that almost defied even their stoic endurance. One has only to run his fingers through the rich black loam of Edisto Island and then wonder how the stolid farmers, the heroic Palatines, scratched an existence· ... and lived.*

*They did. Until most recent years, however, the German Lutherans have been a people who, while not living on the edge of poverty, certainly were not abundant in wealth. Yet, despite the scarcity of worldly goods, they founded three institutions which have served the state, the south and the nation: Newberry College in Newberry, the Lowman Home for the aged in White Rock and the Southern Theological Seminary in Columbia.*

*The stories of their genuinely heroic and warmly human forbearance over the centuries, conveyed to me since last week, are sufficient to prompt a "Tales of the Dutch Fork."*

*During this year, a new history of their church-the Lutheran Synod of South Carolina-is likely to be completed and published. No better time could have been chosen.*

*Uncommonly zealous, uncommonly courageous, uncommonly humble, the German of the Dutch Fork never been a boastful people. They watched their sons and daughters marry and move into the growing community of Columbia and grow more prosperous. They have, always, been a people uncomplaining-except where complaints were just and the grievances extraordinary.*

*They have been there and are there, just as the red clay land was there and is there. The land has been theirs and with their heart and souls, they have built a portion of Carolina. To them, in a birthday year, a state should say, "Well done, thou good and faithful servants."*

# These are a few more details I found out about each Lybrand in the Sam Lybrand Line.

*The following are bits and pieces about each of Sam Lybrand's ancestors and a little bit more about me. Some of these stories came from individuals or distant cousins. Before each of these stories or tales I have identified who they came from to give them full credit for their help in putting together this Lybrand story. Some of the letters or stories have been written down just as the individual wrote them. Under pictures that were sent to me from others I have identified the individual that sent them to me. It is my objective to give full credit to those that have helped me put this Lybrand story together.*

## Wolffgang Leibbrand

*As mentioned before Wolf or Wolffgang Liebbrand was one of the first Lybrand's ever registered in Germany. Therefore 1542 is about as far as I could go back in my search. Some records I found in the internet say he was born in Sweden and died in Germany.*

*His name comes up as an ancestor of many Lybrand's but so far, I have not been able to find out anything about him other than his name.*

## Andreas Leibbrandt

*His name also comes up as an ancestor of many Lybrand's but so far I have not been able to find out anything about him other than his name.*

## Hans-Michael Leuprandt (Leibbrandt) (I've found several other variations for his name.

Hans was employed as "Burgermeister des Gerichs" (Mayor & Judge.) in Kleningersheim (Note Harvie Samuel Lybrand was also 1st Mayor of Edisto Beach.) So far, I have found no Lybrand that has held a political position other than Hans and Harvie.

## Hans Heinrich Leuprandt (Leibbrand)

His name also comes up as an ancestor of many Lybrand's but so far, I have not been able to find out anything about him other than his name.

**Matthias Leibbrandt**

His name also comes up as an ancestor of many Lybrand's but so far, I have not been able to find out anything about him other than his name.

**Rabbit Trail:** It appears that the first four Lybrand's that lived in South Carolina lived close to the Saluda River near Lexington, Chapin and the Gilbert, SC areas. Most of this area is now under Lake Murray that dammed up the Saluda River near Irmo, SC in the late 1920s to the early 1930s. Hendrick lived near the dam and the town of Lexington, SC, Christian lived between Lake Murray and Gilbert, SC and John and John, Jr. lived between Chapin, SC and Lake Murray. In fact, the property the Johns owned fronts on the part of Bear Creek that is under the lake.

Wesley Allen, George Washington and John Samuel Lybrand lived in the Wagener/New Holland, SC area that is southwest of Lexington, SC about 20 to 30 miles away from the town. From what I can find out, Wesley Allen moved there in 1850. Therefore from 1753 to the 1940s all of my ancestors have lived fairly close to each other. This has made it easier to find out more about each of our ancestor. **Back to________**

## Hendrick Lybrand

The first person that I know much about is Hendrick Lybrand. The following is the wording found on the petition, survey and land grant used to get Hendrick Lybrand's 250-acre land grant on the 20-mile branch of the Saluda River. I have a copy of the original land grant and survey but I only have the wording of the petition. I have given the original copy of the land grant and survey to my daughter Amy King.

**Petition of Hendrick Lybrand:**

Petition of Hendrick Lybrand
(Copied from the Council Journal)
Vol. 21, prt 1, page 340

Read the petition of Hendrick Lybrand humbly setting forth that the petitioner came into this province from Germany on the encouragement given him by foreign Protestants and shipped himself and family on board the Ship Elizabeth bound from Rotterdam to this port and has paid his passage money as appears by the enclosed discharge of Mr. John McCall, he is desirous to be a subject of his Majesty King George and to live in this Province. He has a wife and three children Viz Christian aged 28 years, Simon 18 and Maria 16 years for whom not yet for himself has any land been granted, and therefore he humbly prays his excellence and their honors that they would have the Survey General to run out to the Petitioner 250 acres of land free of charges and that he may have his most gracious Majesty's Bounty and the Petitioner as in Duty Bound shall pray.

Charleston Town the 15th day of March 1753.    Hendrick Lybrand

The said petition being considered and the petitioner appearing and swearing allegiance to his Majesty and to the truth of his said petition the prayer thereof was granted, and the Deputy Secretary ordered to prepare a warrant and the Secretary General to lay out the 250 acres of land prayed for that so a grant may issue to the petitioner for the same and that the Commissioner General do pay the charges and the Bounty.

**The Platt (survey) for Hendrick Lybrand**

(It was laid out and drawn up 23 March 1753, and certified 11 September 1753.) Pursuant to a precept to me directed by George Hunter, Esq. Surveyor

General bearing date this 23rd day of March Anno Dom: 1753, I have surveyed and laid out unto Hendrick Lybrand a tract of land containing two Hundred fifty acres, situated lying and being on a branch of Saludy River called the Twenty Mile Branch: butting and bounding to the NW part on vacant land, and part on land laid out to Christopher Keitheimer and part on land laid out to George Cate, and to the NE part on the land laid out to John Gibson, and part land laid out to John George Prock and to the SE part of land laid out to John George Prock, and part vacant, and to the SW part on vacant land, and part on land laid out to Christopher Keitheimer: and hath such shaped form and marks as are represented by the above plot certified by me the 11th day of September AD 1753.

**Land Grant:**

(202) 2tfh October 1753 Detailed by John Gibson

George the Second, by the Grace of God, Of Great Britain, France and Ireland, KING, Defender of the Faith, and so forth, to all to whom These Presents shall come, Greeting: KNOW YE, THAT WE of our special grace, certain knowledge and mere Motion, have given and granted, and by these presents, of us, our heirs and successors, DO GIVE AND GRANT unto **Hendrick Lybrand** his heirs and assign a plantation on track of land containing two hundred and fifty acres on a branch of the Saludy River called the Twenty Mile Branch bounding to the northwestward part of vacant ·land part on land laid out to Christopher Ruthuner's part of land laid out to George Cote and to the northeastward part on land laid out to John Gibson's part on land laid out to John George Prock to the southwestward part on vacant land and part on land laid out to Christopher Ruthuner and hath such shape, form and marks, as appears by a plat thereof annexed: Together with all woods, under-woods, timber and timber-trees, lakes, ponds, fishing's, waters, water- courses, profits commodities, appurtenances and hereditaments whatsoever, thereunto belonging or in anywise appertaining: Together with privilege of hunting, hawking and fowling in an upon the same, and all mines and minerals whatsoever; saving and reserving, nevertheless, to us, our heirs and successors, all white pine trees, if any there should be found growing thereon: And also saving and reserving, to us, our heirs and successors, one tenth-part of mines of silver and gold only: TO HAVE AND TO HOLD, the said Tract of Two Hundred and Fifty acres of land and all and singular other the premises hereby granted, with the appurtenance, unto said **Hendrick Lybrand** heirs and assigns forever, in free and common socage, he the said **Hendrick Lybrand** his heirs or assigns yielding and paying therefore; unto us, our heirs and successors, or to our Receiver-General for the time being, or to his Deputy or Deputies for the time being, yearly, this is to say, on every twenty-fifth day of March, at the rate of three shillings sterling, or four shillings proclamation money, for every hundred acres, and so in proportion according to the quantity of acres, contained herein; the same to grow due and be accounted for from the date hereof. Provided always, and this present Grant is upon condition, nevertheless, that he the said **Hendrick Lybrand** his heirs and assigns, shall and do, within three years next after the date of these presents, clear and cultivate at the rate of one acre for every five hundred acres of land, and so in proportion according to the quantity of acres herein contained; or build a dwelling house thereon, and keep a flock of five head of cattle for every five hundred acres, upon the same, and in proportion for a greater or lesser quantity: And upon condition, that if the said rent, hereby reserved, shall happen to be in arrears and unpaid for the space of three years from the time it became due, and no distress can be found on the said land, tenements, and hereditaments hereby granted; that then and in such case, the said lands, tenements and hereditaments hereby granted, and every part and parcel thereof, shall revert to us, our heirs and successors, as fully and absolutely, as if the same had never been granted. Provided also, If the said lands hereby mentioned to be granted, shall happen to be within the bounds or limits of any of the Townships, or of the land reserved for the use of the Townships now laid out in our said Province, in pursuance of our royal instruction, then this Grant shall be void, anything herein to the contrary contained notwithstanding.

Given under the Great Seal of our said Province Witness his Excellency James Glen

Governor and Commander in chief in and ever our said Province of South Carolina this Twelfth day of February Anno Dom 1755 and in the twenty eighth year of our Reign.


    James (L S) Glen
      Signed by his Excellency in Council
And hath hereunto annexed a Plat
thereof referring the same           Wm Simpson. CC
Certified by George Hunter, Eng
Surveyor-General           The 11th Day of September 1753


It appears that the survey was done in March of 1753 and the Grant was given in February 1755. It appears that you had to live on the land and improve it for two years before you got the grant. As stated, I am attaching a copy of the survey. It is hard to read but the first part of the Land Gant gives a more readable description of the land than the actual survey does. Twenty Mile Branch/Creek of the Saluda is located Between Old Chapin Road and Wise Ferry Road. The Creek runs from just below Old Cherokee Indian Road and runs down into the Saluda River. Old Chapin Road used to cross Twenty Mile Creek just before the bridge that used to cross the Saluda River. Most of Twenty Mile Creek in now under Lake Murray.

I have included a copy of a portrait of Governor James Glen who signed the original land grant.

Here is a little bit about how I got permission to use the Portrait of Governor James Glen. Awhile back I bought Joyce a book called **South Carolina, A History,** by Walter Edgar. When I was thumbing through it I came upon a portrait of Governor James Glen. He was the British Governor at the time Hendrick Lybrand came to Charles Town to get a promised Land Grant. It seemed awfully familiar to me and I wondered why for a day or so. Then I realized that Governor Glen was the man that signed Hendrick Lybrand's Land

Grant. I got excited and wrote Walter Edger for permission to use a copy of the portrait in this book. He wrote back and told me he did not own the portrait and that it belonged to the Earl of Dalhousie. I then went to the internet and found the Earl of Dalhousie's family and wrote them for permission to use the portrait. In a week or so I got an email giving me permission to use the portrait. This is Governor James Glen's portrait. (Before I show Glen's portrait, I want to show a map of Lake Murray and approximately where the first four Lybrand's lived. These are marked with red arrows pointing to the locations.)

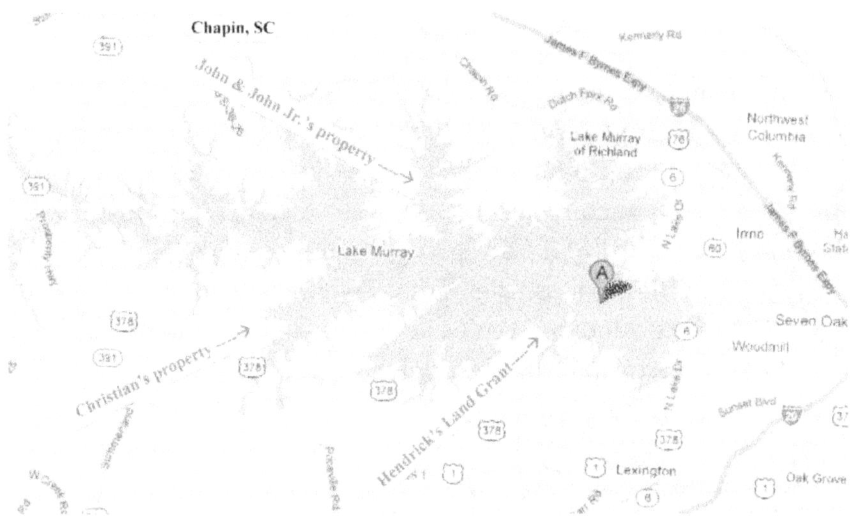


## Why Grants in the middle of the state?

For some time, I have wondered why all these grants were made in the middle of the state. The following from Wikipedia free encyclopedia on the internet explains this when talking about the town or area of Lexington, SC.

*"The historic town of Lexington, South Carolina is a direct descendant of the old Royal township of Saxe Gotha. This township was one of eleven established in 1735 by the Colonial government of King George II to encourage settlements of backcountry South Carolina and serve as a protective buffer between powerful Indian tribes to the west and the older*

*settled plantations of the low county. The name Saxe Gotha was given in honor of the marriage of the King's son, Frederick Louis Prince of Wales, to Princess Augusta of the German Duchy of Saxe-Gotha. (The latter couple became the parents of King George III of England.)*

*The territory of colonial Saxe Gotha covered most of present-day Lexington County and was traversed by two important early Indian trails, the Cherokee Path which followed roughly modern U.S. Highway #378 and the Occaneechi Path, today*

*U.S. Highway #1. These ancient trading paths and the highway that later developed from them have had an enormous impact on the historical development of the area.*

*Most of the early settlers came from various cantons, principalities and city- states of Germany and Switzerland. Others came down from Pennsylvania, and Virginia. Despite the disruption of the Cherokee Indian War of 1760 and the "Regulation" unrest that followed, the township flourished as a largely self-sufficient area of small-scale farming operations. Major crops in the 1s'h Century included corn, wheat tobacco, hemp, flax, beeswax and livestock."*

### Another bit I found on the internet puts it this way:

*"European settlement of this area began around 1718 when the British established a trading post on the Congaree River, which eventually became the town of Granby. Beginning in the 1730s many German, Swiss, and Scots-Irish immigrants moved into the area and established small farms. Granby was the leading town and county seat of Lexington County for many years, but the growth of Columbia across the Congreee lead to Granby's decline, and the county seat was moved to the town of Lexington in 1818."*

### Another bit:

*"The Congaree River has always provided transportation to the up country, up to the rapids at the junction of Broad and Saluda rivers. This location had proven to be a natural spot for a trading center as early as 1718 and the town of Grandy had developed on the western shore of the Congaree River by 1748."*

One question that kept haunting me was, "How did those who received land grants in Charles Town get to the land they were granted?" After looking and looking for the answer I have come to understand that early settlers were blocked by thick forest. The best way to get inland was by river. But this was quite a task going up against the current that was always going south or toward the ocean. Eventually Indian trails were slowly improved into wagon and stagecoach roads. If the settlers were rich enough, they might have ridden on a stagecoach. But I have found no indication that Hendrick was rich.

According to William B. Rauch, (whose family married into the Lybrand's when Hillard Rauch married Mary Lybrand, John N. (Jack) Lybrand's daughter) Hendricks Lybrand went to live with his son Christian Lybrand in his later years and was buried along with his son Christian in the Hollow Creek area, which is up Hwy 378 from Lexington. I understand that this old cemetery is now under Lake Murray and the graves were marked with large stones and not identified. One of the descendants of Christian Lybrand related to William B. Rauch that his ancestors were buried in this old cemetery.

**Christian Lybrand (Liebbrand) Born October 8, 1728 From Doris Brittain:** (A Land Grant to Christian)

*"Pursuant to a warrant to me directing by John Bremar, Esqr, Deputy Surveyor General bearing date the 2 day of March 1773 I have admeasured and laid out unto Christian Librand a plantation or tract of land containing one hundred acres situated in Colleton County on the waters of Saludy River butting and bounding to the SEst on Jacob Harman's land to the Nest on John Young's land the other sides on Vacant land and hath such shape and marks as a plat above represents certified for the 2 day of April 1773 Pr me Pat Cunningham De S."*

One record I found states that Christian moved to Hollow Creek area of South Carolina near the present location of Cedar Grove

James Glen, royal governor of South Carolina (1743–1756), by an unknown artist.
Courtesy of the Earl of Dalhousie.

Church and changed his name to Lybrand. The Hollow Creek area is up the present Hwy. 378 near Gilbert, SC., and not too far away from Lake Murray. There is a Cedar Grove Lutheran Cemetery near this area that confirms the locations given in the first account I found. The Lake Murray map that I mentioned before shows that Hollow Creek is located about six to eight miles up the Saluda River on the Lexington Side of the Saluda River and starts near where it crossed the present Hwy. 378.

Christian Lybrand is buried along with his father in the cemetery just mentioned.

William B. Rauch, which is one of the best historians in the Saluda River area where the first four Lybrand's lived, sent me the following and told me that this is where Hendrick and Christian are buried. This account is part of the records of the cemeteries around the Saluda River area when the Lake Murray Dam area was about to be flooded. He stated that he is sure this is when Hendrick and Christian are buried.

"Unknown Graveyard No. 8 --- Graves marked with rough stones: 8

Letter Aug. 28, 1928 from John J. Long, Gilbert, SC. ".... An old graveyard located on the place bought by you from me. This graveyard has not been used in many, many years. The place has been in possession of my family for about 70 years. I do not know of any living relatives or of the names of anyone buried there. There is another graveyard on the same place said to be a Lybrand graveyard. This too, has not been used in generations, and the only living relative, a distant one, of those buried there whom I know is Mr. Bath Lybrand of Leesville, SC. When I spoke to him about this graveyard a short time ago, he said he did not know anything about it, but that his father had told him that his people came from this section."

# John Lybrand, Sr. - 1760 - August 10, 182?

**From Doris Brittain:**

*A Lybrand woman called Anna received 894 acres of land on Bear Creek in 1808. The wife of John, Sr. is referred to as Anna "the Elder".* This property was down Bear Creek from where John N. (Jack) Lybrand's land was located. There is also an old Lybrand cemetery located near this property. I am not sure who is buried in this cemetery.

I have found from some material I received from the Newberry County Library that John Lybrand, Sr. and his wife Nancy Benay were buried in a Lybrand-Rauch family cemetery near an area outside of Chapin, SC called Fairbanks near the old Koon Store. It is also off Amick's Ferry Road. The cemetery was near Bear Creek which is now under Lake Murray. John N. (Jack) Lybrand and his wife are also buried in this cemetery. There are also five other Lybrand's buried in this old cemetery.

The following information jumps ahead a little but I thought it would be a good place to put it because John, Sr. and John, Jr. are buried in the same cemetery. A write up that I obtained permission to use from the *Dutch Fork Digest, Vol. XXVI - October-November-December 2011 - No 4,* written by William B. Rauch is included on the next two pages. It shows the old Lybrand home site and the family cemetery and who is buried in it. My thanks go out to Mr. Rauch for getting me permission to use this piece of our family history.

Before I get to the layout that Mr. Rauch gave me permission to use, I have included a picture I got from Ancestry.Com that shows a picture of Mary Ann Lybrand Rauch and five generation of Rauch's taken in 1916. As I have already shown, the Rauch's married into the Lybrand clan when a Hillard Rauch married Mary Ann Elizabeth Lybrand, Jack Lybrand's sixth child.

Shown in the picture is Mary Ann Lybrand Rauch with her son, Joseph E. Rauch, her granddaughter, Anne R. Arnold, her great granddaughter, Bessie

A. Frick, and her great-great granddaughter, Mary Evelyn Frick (Fulmer).

I have included this to show how large and diverse a family can get in a few generations. There is no telling how many descendants Hendrick Lybrand now has in South Carolina and all across America. I stopped counting the last names that the whole Hendrick Lybrand family is made up of. I hope we all meet up in heaven.

# JACK (JOHN) LYBRAND PLACE

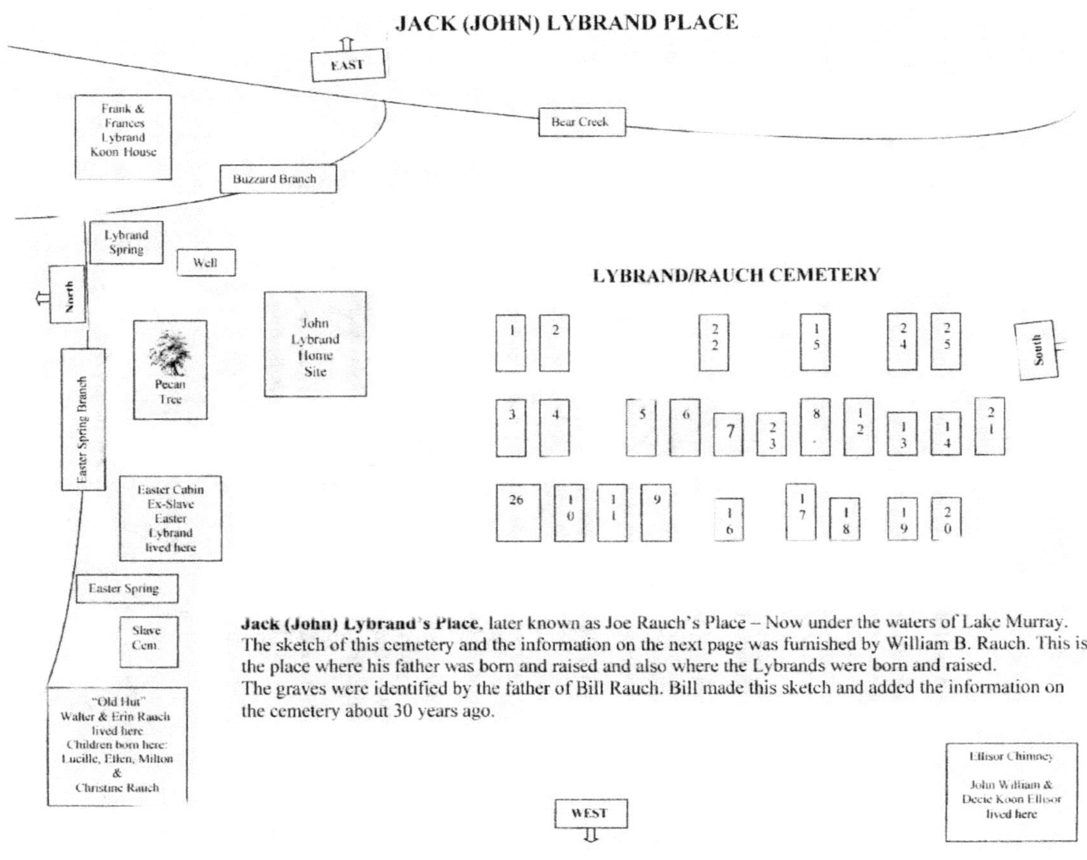



**Jack (John) Lybrand's Place**, later known as Joe Rauch's Place – Now under the waters of Lake Murray. The sketch of this cemetery and the information on the next page was furnished by William B. Rauch. This is the place where his father was born and raised and also where the Lybrands were born and raised. The graves were identified by the father of Bill Rauch. Bill made this sketch and added the information on the cemetery about 30 years ago.

# LYBRAND/RAUCH CEMETERY TRANSCRIPTION

1. John Lybrand. Sr. – Father of Jack
2. Anna Nancy Benay Lybrand – Mother of Jack
3. John (Jack) Lybrand
4. Elizabeth Fulmer Lybrand
5. Joshua E. Lybrand
6. Mary Eve Frazier Lybrand
7. Joshua Luther Lybrand – Son of Joshua
8. John Noah Lybrand – Son of Jack
9. Mary Ann Lybrand Rauch
10. John Jacob (Bub) Rauch
11. Tommy Lee Rauch
12. Lucinda Lybrand Frick
13. Elizabeth Frick
14. Cohen Frick
15. Eberhart Fulmer – Father-in-law of Jack Lybrand
16. Julius Koon – Son of Daniel & JoAnn Rauch Koon - Sister of Joseph Rauch
17. George William Rauch – Husband of Minnie Rauch Leaphart – Moved to St. Johns Lutheran Church, Lexington, SC.
18. Carrie Rauch – Daughter of William & Minnie Rauch – Moved to St. Johns Lutheran Church, Lexington, SC
19. Tillman Derrick - Child of JoAnn Rauch Derrick & Backman Derrick – (Tillman and Bernice Derrick were moved to)
20. Bernice Derrick - Child of JoAnn Rauch Derrick & Backman Derrick – (Red Bank Methodist Church, Lexington, SC)
21. Jesse Leroy Arnold – Brother of Henry Arnold – Henry married Anna Rauch
22. Ann Elizabeth Stingley Lybrand – Born 1823 the first wife of David D. Lybrand. Ann Elizabeth was 16 years old and died in childbirth on September 30, 1839 when her son John Jacob Lybrand was born.  She was a daughter of Jacob and Barbara Derrick Stingley.
23. Joey Rauch – Child of Hilliard and Mary Ann Lybrand Rauch lived one day not baptized
24. George Bauknight – Born 1793 Died 1872
25. Elizabeth Smith Bauknight – born 1-23-1802, Died after 1880 census – The Bauknight's lived not far away - Mr. Bauknight asked Joseph Rauch if they could be buried in the Lybrand/Rauch Cemetery.
26. This was to be gravesites of Joseph and Martha Rauch, but due to Lake Murray being built, they were buried at St. Peters (Piney Woods) Church.

In 1996 when the waters of Lake Murray was lowered, Bill Rauch accompanied several of the Dutch Fork Chapter members to the Lybrand/Rauch Cemetery and the Lybrand home site. Only the bricks from the chimney were visible at the location of the home site.
*The old home made bricks make a great ancestor souvenir when nothing else is left on the site. (SFT)*

Submitted by:  William B. Rauch

**John N. (Jack) Lybrand, Jr. - May 1, 1791 - August 10, 1863 From** Doris Brittain's book:

*"Jack was born 1 May 1791 and married Elizabeth Fulmer 18 February 1813, the family lived on 412 acres of land about four miles south of Chapin, SC on Bear Creek in the Dutch Fork area. They attended St. Peters Piney Wood Lutheran Church, James (Lybrand) Lutheran Church (Note that a section is included on the Lybrand Lutheran Church) and Macedonia Lutheran Church."*

Continued from Doris Brittain:

*"In 1860 John was blind and ill. Joshua and his family moved back to South Carolina from Mississippi after 1860. David was in Texas; Joshua, Wesley (Wesley Allen Lybrand) and John Noah joined the Civil War. Their daughter, Mary Ann Rauch, and her two children, Joseph E and Jo Ann Katherine Elizabeth, moved back and lived with them after her husband Hillard died suddenly in 1859 at Garden Valley Texas, where they lived next to David and his family.*

*According to Jo Ann Katherine Rauch Koon: 'During the Civil War, the raiders came through and confiscated all the food and staples in the house, including a barrel of flour (which they had carefully hidden). As a result, they had to reuse the salt with which they cured meat. They survived by eating beans and potatoes (when available), leaves from trees, and roasted tree leaves for coffee. 'In spite of her grandfather John's blindness and the cruelty of the war, she remembers him as a loving, thoughtful man. He would hold her on his lap, pat her on the head and tease her. She was left with a pleasant, lasting impression toward her grandparents. J.A. K. E. Rauch married James Daniel Koon in S.C. and moved to Sheridan, Arkansas in the late 1800s. Their son, John Jacob Koon, was the father of cousin Joey Koon Walker of North Highlands, CA., who shared this with me,*

*Joshua and John Noah died from dysentery and typhoid during the war. Wesley lost his left arm at the siege of Atlanta. Miss Mary Fulmer must have been a comfort to the family and very dear to them.*

*John died 10 August 1863 and Elizabeth died in 1865."*

The following will information came from Doris Brittain's and Jack Lybrand's book.

## Last Will of John Lybrand, Jr. (John N, (Jack) Lybrand)

(Note that bis will was dictated since it appears that he could not read or write)

*I, John Lybrand of Lexington District and State of South Carolina, being of sound mind and memory and considering the uncertainty of life, and feeling desirous to dispose of such worldly goods as it hath pleased God to bless me with, do hereby make, ordain, publish and declare this to be my last will and testament; that is to say, first my body is to be decently interred, my funeral expenses and all my lawful debts paid and discharged and the residue of my estate, real and personal, I give, bequeath and dispose of as follows to wit. To my beloved wife, the tract of land on which I now reside, containing Three Hundred and Seventy-two acres, lying in District and State aforesaid. Also two slaves Elie and Peggy and also one of my best horses, the choice to be made by her and further two cows and calves, two ewes and lambs and two sows and pigs all to be chosen by herself and lastly one buggy and harness and such of my household and kitchen furniture as she may need and make choices of, and enough corn and flour and fodder as may be necessary to support her and her stock until the gathering of ensuing crop and also as much meat and lard as she may need for the support of herself and two negroes up to the first day of December ensuing. Also one two horse wagon and gears, one thrashing machine, running gear, cog wheel and band for driving the same and all the money (if any) that I may have in cash at the day of my death all of which she is to have, possess and make use of as during her life and after her death to be sold and disposed of as follows - viz, the proceeds of the land to be divided into seven equal shares, one share to my daughter, Rutha, wife of Emanuel Derrick, one share to my son David Lybrand, one share to be equally divided among the seven heirs of my son Joshua Lybrand, deceased, one share to my daughter, Mary Ann, one share to my daughter, Lucinda, one share to my daughter Louisa, and one share to my daughter, Francis share and share alike. My son Westley having already received his portion of land and the proceeds of the Negroes and other property to be equally divided among my eight children. The heirs of my son Joshua Lybrand, deceased, to have (an equal share) that is one eighth to be equally divided among the surviving children (or their heirs) of said John Lybrand, deceased. To my daughter-in-*

*/aw, Mary E. Wife of Joshua Lybrand, deceased, I give forty acres of land, being a part of the tract of land on which I now reside, adjoining said tract on the East and South of d. Efirds land on the West and Koon Land on the North and which is acre fully represented by the dotted lines on a resurvey plat of 413 acres executed by Jasper H. Taylor on the 26 & 27 day of January 1860, to belong to her during her life and after her death to belong to George Washington and Joshua Luther Lybrand jointly and in case of the death of one to belong to the survivor. To my sister-in-law Mary Ann Fulmer, I give and bequeath Fifty Dollars. All the rest residue and remainder of my estate of kind whatsoever, to be sold to the highest bidder and the proceeds to be equally divided among my eight children (the heirs of Joshua Lybrand deceased, receiving the share of their father, Joshua, deceased,) share and share alike.*

*Likewise, I make, constitute and appoint my son Westley Lybrand and my friend John H, Koon, to be executors of this my last will and testament hereby revoking all other wills by me made. In witness whereof I have hereunto subscribed my name and aff,xed my seal (by mark) the seventeenth day of December in the year of our Lord, On Thousand Eight Hundred and Six.ty Two. .*

*John Lybrand*
*XHismark*

*The above written instrument was subscribed by the said John Lybrand in our presence and acknowledged by him to each of us and he at the same time subscribed and declared the above subscribed to be his last will and testament and we as the testers request and in his presence have signed our names as witnesses hereto and written apposite our names our respective place of residence.*

| Thomas Long-His Mark | Lexington District, South Carolina |
| Jacob Koon - His Mark | Lexington District, South Carolina |
| William Ballentine - His Mark | Lexington District, South Carolina |
| Daniel Shealy, Jr. -His Mark | Lexington District, South Carolina |

** Note that John Lybrand, IV and John Noah Lybrand were not mentioned in this will. I cannot find out why. Earlier in Doris Brittain's material she mentioned that Joshua and John Noah died from dysentery and typhoid during the Civil War. As mentioned before over time things are lost in the passing down of information. Plus, some names are spelled differently in different places. I credit this to the fact that many documents were written down like they the sounded as they were given to the person writing things down by the person that could not read or write.

One of the records left by John Jr.'s wife, Elizabeth, after John's death showed, according to Doris Brittain, that she had three slaves, her most valuable possession. Their names and Elizabeth's estimate of value were.

"Bill & Easter    $500.00
Ellick           $650.00
Peggy            $500.00"

I've look far and wide and not been able to find out what happened to these slaves. Of course, they were freed shortly after both John and Elizabeth died.

After Elizabeth died, Wesley Allen Lybrand, John and Elizabeth's son, bought the slaves called Bill, Easter and Ellick in April 1865. Peggy was bought that same date by Mary Ann Rauch. These dates do not make sense. I could not find out why these slaves were bought after they were officially freed by the results of the Civil War.

William (Bill) Rauch related to me that the slave, Easter Lybrand, did not leave. In the1870 Lexington County census Easter is living next to the Rauch's and had a four-year-old male child named West with her. He related that he did not know if West was her child or not. At the time of this census Easter was 44 years old.

He also related that there was one black Lybrand named Robert Lybrand who tended the Wise Ferry across the Saluda River between Chapin and Lexington. Robert is mentioned in several publications **(Lake Murray Land and Leisure)** for one, and gives a good report on him. He played the harmonica for the passengers and also told them interesting stories.

Bill told this story about a ferry crossing. I am not sure if he was relating it about Robert Lybrand or not. "In about 1908 my father's sister, Minnie Rauch, and her husband, George William Rauch, who lived on the south side of Saluda River in about 1908 bought a new automobile. They were coming to visit her parents at the Lybrand - Rauch place. When they had crossed the Saluda on the barge (ferry) and gotten to the other side, instead of waiting until the ferry was tied tightly, George put his car in gear and spun the ferry backwards out from under the car, leaving them in the water up to their neck. The motor in the new car was ruined when the hot engine hit the cold water."

He also told me that he has knowledge of several blacks with the name of Lybrand during the time after the Civil War. He also told me that he knows of several blacks in the Columbia, Lexington area but did not feel right about asking them about their heritage as related to the Lybrand's. He also said that he knew of some blacks that also had slaves.

To say the least this was an interesting but hard time around the Civil War days.

As I went through what I could find out about John (Jack) Lybrand, Jr., references to St. James (Lybrand) Lutheran Church kept coming up. Therefore, this is some of which I found.


**St. James Lutheran Church (Lybrand Lutheran Church**) (The old church's location is now under Lake Murray.)

The following is from Doris Lybrand's book.

*"Henry Lybrand deeded one acre of his property to the Elders of this church January 1821. (Deed Book 1, page 637, Court Clerk's Office, Lexington, SC.) The residents living below Pine Ridge built the church*

*near the banks of Bear Creek. Rev. John Lybrand, Jesse Lowman and students from the Lexington Theological School served the congregation of this building which was still partly standing when Lake Murray was built. (1929-1930 approx.) It was cleared away by the Lake Murray Project.*

*It was a neat church with goblet-like pulpit over which hung a large and beautiful sounding board, carved and painted, a work of art, handmade. Among those who worshipped and were members were: The Ballentines, Hillers, Haltiwangers, Shealys, Longs and Lybrands.*

*The history of the Lybrand Church is wrapped in considerable obscurity, but we are not in doubt as to its birthplace and the cause that gave rise to its organization. The church was built of hewn logs about 20 x 40 feet."* (According to Doris Britain, these last two paragraphs came from St. Peter's Church records.)

Another story from Doris Brittain's book

*"Mr. Willie A. Wessinger remembered that Dr. Soloman Haltiwanger told him that "One summer during a very long dry spell, the members had met on a week day to pray for rain. He (Dr. Sol) rode on a horse behind his aunt. As they were going home, everyone got soaking wet from the rain."*

The following St. James Lybrand Lutheran Church history was written by William B. Rauch and appeared in the Dutch Fork Digest in the July-Aug. Sep. issue of 2002:

"The St James (Lybrand) Church"

*"On January 1, 1821 Henry Lybrand deeded to the Elders of St. James (Lybrand) church I acre of land, surrounded on all sides by land of Henry Lybrand. The Church was probably already built at this time. The location of the Church was on the southern edge of Doc. Hamilton's Point, near the Timberlake Plantation. There are graves there (1 grave marked and 14 marked with rough stones when Lake Murray was built) The marked grave is for George Lybrand born 1798 died 1848. The Known Graves are:*

*1.    George Lybrand 1781-1848 (Henry Lybrand's son)*

*2.    Henry Lybrand ca. 1765-1837 (John Lybrand, Sr.'s Son)*

*3.    Mary Barbara Ballentine Lybrand ca. 1770-1842- Wife of Henry Lybrand*

4. *William Haltiwanger 1803-1878*

5. *Kesiah Lybrand Haltiwanger 1808-1873*

6. *Annie Coogler ca. 1875-1880*

7. *Daniel Lybrand ca 1795 -1818 Son of Henry and Barbara*

8. Male Lybrand Child name unknown ca. 1793-180? Son of Henry and Barbara

9. Male Lybrand Child name unknown ca 1795-180? Son of Henry and Barbara

(From another source.)

10. Eberhardt Fulmer, Jack Lybrand's father-in-law 1770-1843

11. Joshua Lybrand and his wife

12. David Lybrand (brother of Wesley Allen) and first wife Anna Elizabeth Lybrand

My grandmother told me that the grave of Kisiah Haltiwanger was robbed by grave robbers and they left the body on top of the ground. They were never caught/or this. In those days many valuables were buried with the bodies. The body of Anna Coogler was moved to Bethel Lutheran Cemetery at White Rock.

When the Lake Murray water level is at 362, the Cemetery is covered, but the location where the Church stood is above water. The church is described as being 20 by 40 feet, but in 1960 the corner stones were still there, and measure 24 by 40 feet. The church was built of hewn logs and was described as a neat building. There were two doors, on the north side and one on the east end. It has a goblet-like Pulpit over which hung a large sounding board. The sounding board was made in the shape of a star and painted Red.

The Church was used as a place of worship until after 187-. About 1890 when my father Walter. E. Rauch was 8 years old, the church was still standing, but the roof had fallen in. He and his brothers and friends would pass the location going to Saluda River to fish.

The church was Lutheran and in 1842 was served by Rev. Herman Aull. Rev. Jesse Lowman and Rev. Godfrey Dreher were also known to preach there. The Church was abandoned probably due to the establishment of Macedonia Church in 1847. Also, many of the older members had died by the 1870's. The building was surely in a poor condition by that time.

The home of Henry Lybrand was located approximately 150 yard east of the Church. It has been said that some of the stones for pillars, chimney, etc. are visible when the water is very low. The church Cemetery must have been as a Lybrand Family Cemetery, since Henry had two sons who died before the Census of 1820. This would be before the Church was built"

The following came from *A History of the Lutheran Church in South Carolina*, published in 1971.

*"St. James (Lybrand), Lexington County."*
*(Near Little Mountain, SC)*

*The first we hear of this church is in the Minutes of the Synod, 1827, when it is listed as a contributor. We are told there that the church was in Lexington District. In 1823 George Lybrand was a lay delegate to the Synod from St James, Lexington District, and St Paul's Newberry District which churches, along with St. Mark's Edgefield District. Petitioned that convention for the services of John C. Hope, then a licientate anticipating study at Gettysburg Seminary. In 1823 St. James asked the services of Levi Badenbaugh, but this petition was denied because Mr. Badenbaugh had just entered the Seminary.*

At any rate, the church must have disbanded before 1847, as the newly organized Macedonia Lutheran Church worshipped then/or a short time in a building called Lybrand's Church.

The following paragraphs come from a history written by the Rev. A.W. Ballentine.

*It must have been about the year 1830 when the Lybrand Church was established. In 1842 the South Carolina Synod met in St. Mark Church, 'Edgefield District', now Saluda County. In the Minutes of the Synod for the year, page 40, mention is made of the Lybrand Church and it is designated in this way, 'St. James (Lybrand) Church'. At that time, it was served by the Rev. George Haltiwanger, Sr. The congregation is mentioned in connection with contributions made to "The Centenary Fund' of the*

*Synod. The names of the contributors as given in the report are: Dr. P.H. Todd, Jeremiah Drehr, Hezekiah Drehr, Jno. M. Sultan (perhaps Mike Sulton), Jacob Bates, Mrs. Singly and Mrs. Jacob Harman. This is the only historic record we have been able to find on the 'Lybrand' Church.*

*The 'Lybrand" Church stood on an elevated place of ground about five miles east of the present Macedonia Church. It was north of the Saluda River and west of bear Creek, less than one mile from the confluence of the two streams. The author of this sketch remembers from boyhood days the location, the remains of an old log building, and some graves marked by stones and boards. When the dam for Lake Murray was built, all the remains of this old church were cleared away, and the spot is covered with the waters of Lake Murray.*

*The History of St. Peter's Church, Piney Woods, Page 24 carries this record, which will be of interest to many: "The church was built of hewn logs about 20 x 40 feet. It was a neat church with a goblet-like pulpit over which hung a large and beautiful sounding board, carved and painted, a work of art - hand made.*

*Pastor A. W. Ballentine states that the building may have been "used as a place of worship as late as the year 1870." Quote from ' History of Macedonia Evangelical Lutheran Church, 1847-1947", Page 4, the Rev. A.W. Ballentine.*

*Pastors who evidently served St. James: J. Hermon Aull, 1836; G. Haltiwanger, Sr., circa 1842."*

The reason I mentioned the Lybrand Lutheran church so much is because it may have been one of the first Lutheran churches built in the Lexington area. Plus, it pleases me that my family was so involved in their Christian beliefs. In Hendrick Lybrand's petitions for a land grant it states that he was a Protestant. You will find that, throughout the Lybrand history, our people's involvement in the Christian Church is often mentioned.

There is a large stone memorial placed in the St. Peters Lutheran Church cemetery that gives a list of those buried in St. James (Lybrand) Lutheran Church. This Lutheran church is located outside of Chapin, SC. There are several Lybrand's named on this memorial.

**Macedonia Church:**

The Macedonia Lutheran Church is also mentioned many times in what I have found in the material I found about the Lybrand's. I have been to the grounds of this church. It is a beautiful white church overlooking Lake Murray. I understand it is located near (about five miles away) where the old Lybrand Lutheran Church was located. The following is from Doris Brittain's Book.

*"John and Elizabeth Lybrand attended this and the Lybrand church until the trouble in 1847 when about twenty-five members on the encouragement of Jack Harmon, Jacob Hiller and Jack Lybrand withdrew and formed Macedonia Church."* I have confirmed this fact with a current historian that now is a member of the Macedonia Church. The historian for Macedonia Lutheran Church also told me that Jack Lybrand was one of the members who paid to have the land surveyed on which Macedonia Church was built. The church records also indicated that a Lybrand was a charter member.

It has been satisfying to me when I have been able to verify facts from more than one source. The following came from St. Peter's Church history.

*"In St. Peter's (Piney Woods) Church History, page 23, Judge C.M. Efird has written as follows; 'Finally, in 1847, some twenty-five members, led by Jack Harman, Jacob Hiller, and Jack Lybrand, withdrew and formed Macedonia Church.'"*

The following is a paragraph from the Macedonia Evangelical Lutheran Church I got off the internet.

*"When the waters of Lake Murray began to rise in 1928, they covered all the roads but one leading to the church and forced many members to leave the area and settle elsewhere. Thus, the membership was reduced to about one-third of its highest enrollment. But the faithful few held on and their numbers gradually grew so that the congregation is now self-supporting."*

The above goes along with the members of St. James (Lybrand) Lutheran Church leaving to form the Macedonia Church. What pleases me the most is finding out that my ancestors regularly attended church.

## Wesley Allen Lybrand -January 92 1823-April 11, 1908
## (Lived 85 years)

Wesley Allen Lybrand,
4th Child of John Lybrand and Sarah Elizabeth Fulmer

Wesley Allen Lybrand, (* Jan. 9, 1823, t April 11, 1908) and his wife, Sarah Elizabeth (Salley) Derrick, (* February 11, 1826, t March 25, 1907).

## Wesley Allen Lybrand and Sarah Elizabeth (Sally) Derrick's Tombstone

(This is the oldest tombstone in the New Holland Cemetery. It was originally the family cemetery for the Lybrand's. Wesley Allen Lybrand's home place is across the road from this old cemetery.)

These words are inscribed on the back of his tombstone: *"Amiable and beloved father and mother farewell. Not on this perishing stone but in the Book of Life, and in the hearts of thy afflicted children is thy worth recorded."*

# --Shirley's Extra --

Sometime after I thought I had exhausted all the information I could find about my direct Lybrand line; I received the following information from Shirley F. Trotter, a distant cousin that branched off from Wesley Allen Lybrand. Therefore, we have in common Wesley Allen Lybrand and all the Lybrand's that came before him.

The following are two letters, one written by Wesley Allen Lybrand during the Civil War, and the other written by his daughter Amanda Lybrand. These letters were written by hand and are very hard to read. Shirley did her best in transcribing them, using the exact words and spelling as was on these letters. I have included these because they give real live thoughts of my direct ancestors and make them come alive. They are not just a names or stories I have been able to collect. These are really their words from around 150 years ago. It appears the letter from Wesley Allen was written before he was wounded in the Civil War. The second one was written by his daughter while he was in the hospital. I understand he was in an Augusta. GA. hospital after he was wounded in the battle of Atlanta.

## Letter - W.A. Lybrand

So. Ca. Lexington Dist. June 13, 186?

Dear Mother and sisters, friends and relatives,

This is to inform you that I arrived safe at home that same evening about dark that I left your house and found all tollera well. I am at home yet but I report to leave for camp tomorrow morning if nothing happens more than common and this is to bid you all farewell. I would like to stay longer but I don't think that I can stay any longer so farewell. I would of bin glad to hear from you all again once more before I leave and I should like to know how you all get along with your crops and wheat for I tell you that we get along but slow for there is so much rain that it looks like the grass will take some of our crops and will get along very slow on cutting wheat for it is not bin ripe until now and to day I thought we would cut a good deal but it rained and knocked us out of cutting much. My wheat is tolerable good. I think if we could save it but now I have to leave and what will become of hit I don't no. I have been up to Mr. Krepeses and Cousin Rubin and they was all tolerable well and old but is moved to cousin Levis and July Lott, Daniel Younces oldest daughter is dead. She went to Georgia to see her husband and she taken____died there.

This leaves us all up except Amanda. She has been lying nearly all day but I believe that it is nothing serious the matter with her and the rest of us has bad coles. I have not bin shed of the cold since I have got home, so I must close by asking you to right to us or to my people until you can find out where to right to me so fare well.

Dear Mother. You said that I should look if B. miller got a hamer at the sail yes, thou None charged to him.

Your - W.A. Lybrand

The following is the other letter Shirley F. Trotter sent me on the same date. It is a hand written letter that was also hard to read. But if you follow along you will get the idea of the letter. Remember both of these letters were written during the Civil War and it is surprising that they have survived this long. Amanda Lybrand was Wesley Allen Lybrand's daughter.

Letter Amanda Lybrand wrote to her Grandmother, Mrs. Elizabeth Lybrand

South Carolina Lexington Dist. September 2, _____
Dear Grandmother and family. I take pen in hand to drop you a few lines to let you no the misfortune that Pa happened the 7 of August. He was setting on the breast works and a shell came in threw the top of the breastwork and hit him on the left hand and rist breaking the bone and bursing the fib. The Dr taken it off betwixt the hand and elbow and after it was taken off he came to

and now over in hospital. Staid there until last Wednesday he came home he is doing

very well now if the c                  broke out it is nearly heald up and don't pain mutch no

more. He can be up Some while I was up there Ma had got letter from him and She has gone to him tel I got back. I tell you that I was glad to See Pa come home as well as well as he did althought it is bad enuf to loose one hand but thank god that it is no worse. The rest of us is well and I truly hope that these few lines may reach you Safe and find you all well. We have pulled some Fodder but the weather is very dry here yet I will tell you that Pa got a very good stomach to eat and it agees with him verry well only his bowels is too loose and I fear that they will pleg him a good while but as long as his is as peart as he is and hope it wont be long be fore he will be well he looks bad but he Ses he is hever than he was when he got wounded for he was Puny So long before he got wounded tel he had fel away to nothing all most. I will close my Short letter for this time hoping to hear from you Soon rite Soon and let us no how you are all doing So no more but Yours as ever Amanda C. Lybrand


Envelope Gunter Store SC Sept 3rd

To:
Mrs. Elizabeth Lybrand Frog Level Newberry Dist SC
In care of A.W. Wheeler in haste

Note:
Elizabeth Lybrand was Wesley Allen Lybrand's wife.


To follow along with the material Shirley sent to me, the following is a picture of Wesley Allen Lybrand's daughter, Frances Permelia Lybrand, and her husband Leroy F. Boatwright.

Before I show the picture, here is another interesting fact. Shirley's mother married Kohan L. Johnson in 1932 and moved to New Holland. Her mother remembered that there were many

Confederate Veterans in uniform at George Washington Lybrand's funeral. He died June 5, 1935.

This is Shirley's ancestry as she related it to me. My son, (John E. Trotter, Jr.)

Me, John and Shirley Trotter

My parents, (Kohan L. and Effie Mae Waters Johnson)

My grandparents, (Jasper Claude and Annie Elizabeth Boatwright Johnson)

My great grandparents, (Leroy F. and Frances Permelia Lybrand Boatwright)

My great, great grandparents, (Wesley Allen and Sarah Elizabeth Derrick Lybrand) All are buried in the New Holland, SC Cemetery.

I have included this to show how the Lybrand blood line has expanded in only a few generations. Shirley and I branch off from Wesley Allen Lybrand. We are about the same age.

In comparison my ancestry runs like this: (Note that Shirley's ancestors have several last names. Ours is unique in that all of our male ancestors have the same last name.)

My grandsons, (**Samuel** Dupree **Lybrand** and John Daniel Hay Lybrand) My sons, (James **Samuel** and John Myers **Lybrand**)

Me, (George **Samuel** and Ida Myers **Lybrand**)

My parents, (Harvie **Samuel** and Jennie 0. **Lybrand**)

My grandparents, (John **Samuel** and Mamie Clayton **Lybrand**)

My great grandparents, (George Washington and Sara Jane Jackson Lybrand)

My great, great grandparents, (Wesley Allen and Sarah Elizabeth Derrick Lybrand) Note that in my line there have been five Sam's in a row with no juniors.

Permelia, whose picture I have below, is George Washington Lybrand's sister.

She is also shown in the picture of Jane Jackson Lybrand, George Washington Lybrand's wife and several other ladies sitting around smoking pipes.

The following is an article out of the State paper published on December 9, 1930. It is about Louisa Selinda Lybrand who married Henry Matthias Wessinger and lived over 100 years. She was the daughter of John N. (Jack) Lybrand and the sister of Wesley Allen Lybrand and Mary Ann Elizabeth Lybrand. She was born December 9, 1830 and died at the ripe old age of 102 on March 5, 1933.

### One Hundredth Birthday Celebration
### At Lowman Home Draws Many Visitors

### Mrs. Louisa Wessinger Welcomes Guests
### In Joyful Manner as 100 Candles
### Shine About Her.
### Services at New Bethel Church.

#### By Jesse Rutledge

Celebrating the 100th birthday of its oldest resident, Mrs. Louisa Wessinger the Lowman home threw open its doors yesterday to hundreds of visitors who came from many parts in the state to take part in the festivities planned in her honor.

Sitting in her large armchair at the center of the reception room of the home while 100 brightly burning candles gleamed about her. Mrs. Wessinger welcomed the visitors and shook hands with every one who desired to speak with her. "There are a lot of people here today and I'm glad of it too," she said in a pleased and joyful tone. Many beautiful gifts reached her during the day. Some of her friends presented money, others clothes, and in connection with the celebration a handsome radio receiving set was given by St. Paul's Lutheran church of Columbia.

Mrs. Wessinger was present in her first silk dress, an attractive black outfit bought a few days ago for the occasion. Over this she wore a black coat.

Mrs. Wessinger was able to walk but due to her weak eyesight and the danger of stumbling and falling, she was usually supported by others when attempting to get from place to place. From her room at the home she walked to an automobile and rode to Bethel church several hundred feet away where services were held in her honor. It was there that Mrs. Julia Aull, who has already celebrated her 99th birthday, was introduced. She lives in Columbia with her daughter, Mrs. W. W. Daniel.

In the beautiful new brick church, completed only a few days previous of the birthday celebration, many words of tribute were paid to Mrs. Wessinger for her long life of service and loyalty. Dr. W. H. Greever, a professor at Columbia Lutheran Theological seminary, gave a short address in which he spoke of time, saying that it is "just a little bit of eternity."

"God doesn't make the distinction of time that we do. Ho recognizes it just as an introduction for us to eternity."

Dr. John D. Long, pastor of the church, paid tribute to Mrs. Wessinger for her loyalty and faithfulness and said that he was glad that the Lutherans had provided such a fine place as the Lowman home for those who are old and unable to care for themselves.

The Rev. V. L. Fulmer of Johnston, whose grandmother was a sister of Mrs. Wessinger and whom he said lived to be 98 years old, gave a short sketch of the family history. Her father, he said was John (Jack) Lybrand and lived for many years in the Dutch Fork section where Mrs. Wessinger was born.

Of the five children born to her, she has three living. Rufus Wessinger of near Chapin, Vastine Wessinger, and Mrs. Jonnna Ballentine of Columbia. Rufus Wessinger was unable to be present because of illness but the others were as well as members of the fifth generation of the family.

During the morning Mrs. Wessinger was carried to the home of C. E. Hotinger superintendant of the institution, where she heard her name and achievements mentioned over the Columbia Broadcasting system of radio station. Three hearty cheers were sounded from the loud speaker.

After services at the church lunch was spread in the dining room of the home, the guest themselves bringing baskets of prepared food.

## PASSES CENTURY MARK

Photo by Sargeant

#### MRS. LOUISA WESSINGER.
Last Tuesday, at Lowman home, near Columbia, Mrs. Wessinger celebrated her 100th birthday, with elaborate ceremonies in her honor.

This article appeared in the State Newspaper on December 9, 1930

Submitted By: Shirley F. Trotter

The picture on the left is of **Mary Ann Elizabeth Lybrand** who married Hillard Rauch. She was the daughter of John N. (Jack) Lybrand. Born 1825, Died 1919.

The picture below is of **Sarah Alice Lybrand**. She married Wilson Uriah Wessinger. She is the daughter of Wesley Allen Lybrand. She is the sister of France Permelia Lybrand Boatwright and George Washington Lybrand. Born 1864, Died 1945. It is not known who the child is.

As I worked on my line of the Lybrand's it was surprising where the material in this book came from. Here are a few items of interest.

Shirley is that State Representative for the **Dutch Fork Chapter of SCGS, Inc**. I wrote the chapter asking for information on my ancestors and she somehow got my letter and since she also came from one of my ancestors, Wesley Allen Lybrand, she responded and began to send me the information and pictures presented in this section I have called **Shirley's Extra**. William B. Rauch, the President of this chapter has also sent me material that I have presented in another section of this book.

Here are a few other interesting items she mentioned as she sent this material to me over several days in about 5 or 6 emails.

*My youngest son was working at Quincy's Steak House when he was in high school in the 80's.*

*One of the young ladies who worked there was his age and used to visit us. The Lybrand name came up and she said she had a grandmother way back who was a Lybrand. She brought me the photo and I had a negative made of it." (This is the picture of Mary Ann Lybrand Rauch Shirley sent me.)*

The plot thickens:

*Just a little bit of information you may not know but do not put this in your book. Alice Lybrand married Wilson Uriah Wesseinger. He was her first Cousin. Wilson's mother was Louisa C. Lybrand Wessinger, A sister to Wesley Allen Lybrand. Louisa is the one I sent you that celebrated her 10th birthday.*

*In one of your emails awhile back you mentioned the New Holland cemetery. I think people have looked for a deed where Wesley donated the land for a cemetery. But I do not think anyone has found a deed with Wesley donating the land for this cemetery.*

*The cemetery is located on that 700 or so tract of land that Wesley purchased from Matthew Ready. I think it was Wesley's first purchased in the New Holland area. If I remember correctly these are some Ready's buried there who were buried there before Wesley Purchased the land. I have wondered if it was a Ready cemetery at the beginning. (From me: I understand that this cemetery was originally the Lybrand family cemetery. At least Wesley Allen Lybrand's grave is one of the oldest graves, if not the oldest.)*

Bits and pieces about the Lybrand's make them come alive and not just a name with a date they were born and a date they died. Therefore, I have included all sorts of information that I have gained from many sources in hopes that in future generations many will know of the contributions the Lybrand's have made and lives they have lived.

Thanks gain to Shirley F. Trotter for her contribution to this story about the Lybrand's.

LYBRAND
JAN. 9, 1823
APR. 14, 1908
FATHER
SARAH DERRICK
WIFE OF
W. L. LYBRAND
FEB. 11, 1826
MAR. 25, 1907
MOTHER
LYBRAND

When you read stories of your distant relatives you have to wonder if they were really real people. But when you see their tombstones and all the dates match, they become real in your mind. Here is a picture of Manervia Lybrand Huckabee, one of Wesley Allen's daughters.

Wesley Allen moved the family to the New Holland, Wagener area in 1850. From what I can find out, he and his wife had 14 children. Of these 10 lived to adulthood. His father, John N. (Jack) Lybrand, Jr., made him executor of his will.

According to my father, Wesley Allen Lybrand owned around 2000 acres in the Wagener, New Holland area and was a very rich man.

One record I got from Jack Lybrand's book gives an idea of the extent of the land Wesley Allen Lybrand bought and how early he started his move to the New Holland, SC area. This is what I found.

*"Recorded 14th May 1947, John Fox, Regr. Delivered to W. A. Lybrand Aug. 7th 1847*

*After Wesley left the Dutch Fork Section of Lexington District, he moved to the New Holland section of Lexington District, now located in Aiken County. He purchased 756 acres of land from Matthew Ready for $3.50 per acre ($2646.00). This parcel of land almost completely encompassed what is now known as the New Holland Community."*

From what I can find out, Wesley Allen continued buying and selling land until a few years before his death in 1908. My father was around four years old at the time and he told me that he vaguely remembers his grandfather lying in state in one of the bedrooms of his home before he was buried.

It appears that all his children were born in the New Holland area.

One of the strange things about Wesley Allen is that he was executor of his father's detailed will and yet he died intestate (with no will). At the time of his death the following claimed to be his heirs and divided his estate and vast amount of property. These heirs were: (I'll try to explain who all these people were.)

Amanda C. Gunter - His daughter - She married Daniel B. Gunter

G.W. Lybrand- His son and my father's grandfather

John W. Lybrand - His son

Jacob W. Lybrand - His son

Alice Wessinger - His Daughter

Manervia Huckabee - His daughter

Joanner Swartz - Descendent of Louisa Joan Lybrand who married Paul Swartz

Permelia Boatwright - His granddaughter

Oscar Lybrand - His grandson

W.F. Lybrand - His son

According to Doris Brittain, here are some reasons he may have moved his family and a little bit about his family.

*"With more children perhaps, more land was needed and the proceeds of the sale of land in the more expensive Columbia area may have been used to buy much more land in the New Holland area.*

*This move may have been made as the Civil War approached or immediately following. There could have been political, family safety, or religious overtones.*

*One of the most tragic, and courageous, stories I have ever heard concerned Willie's young brother, Noah Webster Lybrand (one of Wesley Allen Lybrand' s sons). In 1882, at the age of 23, he was bitten by a rabid dog. At that time, there was no treatment for cure for rabies. He called the family together and told them that he knew that there was nothing that could be done for him and that he would die. He also said that he didn't want to hurt anyone else and the death was something that other members of the family would not want to witness. He asked that they take him some distance away from the home, tie him securely to a tree, leave him some water and let him die, alone. This was done. It certainly represents a degree of courage, reality and concern for others that would rarely, if ever, be duplicated.*

*Wesley Allen and his wife Sarah not only had fourteen children, but the 10 who lived beyond 12 years had an average life span of 67.5 years. This included one who died at 23 of rabies. Wesley lived for 85 years and Sarah lived for 81 years."*

As I was searching Lybrand's that served in the Civil War, I came across this statement under the Schwartz family. "I was told that W.A. Lybrand owned nearly all of Wagener and all the land toward New Holland, SC." I looked a little further and found that Paul William Arthur Schwartz, born May 30, 1858 and died in 1913, met

Manervia Caroline Lybrand, daughter of Wesley Allen Lybrand and Sarah Derrick Lybrand. He married Louisa Joanner Lybrand February 25, 1883, daughter of Wesley and Sarah Derrick Lybrand." This did not make much sense. I looked a little further and found this statement. "As I remember what was told to me was that Paul Swartz came to Wagener to work for W.A. Lybrand in his stores. I was told that W.A. Lybrand owned nearly all of Wagener and all the land between Wagener and New Holland and had stores that carried groceries, clothes, hardware, etc. and he had a livery stable. Mama said Paul Swartz was a very handsome man. Edith told me that Paul Swartz had both Manervia and Joanner pregnant and that

W.A. Lybrand told him that he had to marry one or the other. He chose Joanner.

Then Manervia married Furman Huckabee. I've always wondered why he married her with three illegitimate children. Maybe he married her for what he thought he would get when Manervia's father died. I was told that Wesley Allen Lybrand left each of his children two hundred acres." This shows that human behavior has not changed. Man is not all good and man is not all bad. We are all sinners in God's sight saved by our belief in Jesus Christ.

The fact that he left or intended to leave 200 acres to each of his children confirms the fact that he must have owned 2000 acres in this area.

While I was taking pictures of my ancestors in the New Holland graveyard, I came across the grave of Manervia buried near her father, Wesley Allen Lybrand. While reading about her I had a tendency to think that what I was reading about her was some kind of tale. But when I discovered her grave, I realized that she was a real person.

One cute story I found in Doris Brittain's book gives a little insight into Wesley Allen's character. It goes like this: One of Wesley Allen's grandsons likes to tell of the winter his grandfather asked him to stay with him and work after school and on weekends. If he would do this, Grandfather said he would make it "worth his while". He did this work and when the year was up Grandfather gave him a silver dollar and a red rooster and told him to put them "where they would make more."

Another story about Wesley Allen Lybrand was recorded in Jack Lybrand's book and is listed below. It is talking about a story Jack's father (George Washington Lybrand's son Fred C. Lybrand) told him.

*"I remember one story that Daddy used to tell that I have never forgotten. It seems that when he was a small boy, he went to visit his Grandfather, Wesley A. Lybrand. Back them a lot of the houses were built up off the ground quite a ways and so was the house that Wesley lived in. My father was playing under the house and found a penny. He said that he was so proud of the penny that he went running into the house hollering, 'Grand-daddy, Grand-daddy, I found a penny'. Whereupon his grandfather took the penny from him and looked at it real close, then rubbed it on his pants leg and said 'A LORD SON, PENNIES MAKE DOLLARS' Then put the penny in "His" pocket Daddy said. 'I never did like that old man after that."'*

The Civil War records record that Wesley Allen Lybrand was 40 years old when he was wounded at Atlanta, GA. Family lore says that he was in one battle of Atlanta and lost or had his arm cut off. The picture of him shows that he only had one arm. The battle of Atlanta was fought on July 22, 1864. If you add 40 years to Wesley Allen's birthday the age that the Civil War records give come very close.

The following is an account given by Emily Lybrand. I don't know how she fits into the Lybrand clan. This came off the internet under Lexington, SC Civil War history.

*"Emily Lybrand was born in 1811. She often talked about the tragic days of war. The ruthless Union army had no remorse. They took everything they could get while invading towns. The soldiers took every supply they could get their hands on. They would take the molasses, sauerkraut and other useful items and dump them on the ground. To make sure it could not be saved, soldiers threw dirt on top of it. The union had no mercy and destroyed everything the South ever had. Lybrand lived to*

*tell about it and shared her stories all around." (This was also included in this article: "Sherman's army marches into South Carolina and Lexington County February 1865.")*

Since Wesley Allen Lybrand served in the Civil War, I thought it might be nice to see how many Lybrand's I could find that also served in the Civil War. The following is the list I found and the information that came with what I found. I did not take time to find out how each of these fits into our Lybrand clan. But I am sure most, if not all, are descendants of Hendrick Lybrand.

- *Reuben Lybrand, killed in 1862
- John P. Lybrand born 1839 Died 1920 - member of the 31st Alabama CompanyK
- SC 19th Infantry Regiment, Company A
    - o Captain L. Lybrand
    - o Levi Lybrand, First Lieutenant, age 48; promoted from Second to First Lieutenant February, 1862; resigned 1863
    - o *H. Elsey Lybrand, age 22, Sergeant; Wounded at Chickamauga; died of wounds in hospital
    - o George Lybrand, Age 17, Private
    - o *Martin Lybrand, Age 17, Private, killed in Battle at Atlanta, Ga.
    - o <u>Wesley Allen Lybrand, Age 40, Private, wounded at Atlanta. GA.</u>
    - o From this company 15 killed in battle, 6 mortally wounded, 23 died of disease, 44 total deaths. 13 wounded not mortally; for a total of 57 casualties.
- *John Noah Lybrand died June 1, 1862 - son of John N. (Jack) Lybrand brother of Wesley Allen Lybrand - but does not show up in SC 19th Infantry Regiment, Company A with his brother. As mentioned under John N. (Jack) Lybrand, Doris Brittain's material states that he died of dysentery and typhoid.

- *Joshua E. Lybrand as died of dysentery and typhoid in the Civil war. Therefore, Wesley Allen lost two brothers in the Civil War and was wounded himself.

**Rabbit Trail:** Fate has a great deal to do with our very existence. By a streak of good luck George Washington Lybrand was born before the Civil War. If Wesley Allen Lybrand had not had George Washington before he went into the Civil War and was killed instead of being wounded like his two brothers, the Sam Lybrand line would have not have come into being. **Back to**

- Samuel Lybrand, 20th Regiment, SC Infantry
- Simeon R. Lybrand, 20th Regiment, SC Infantry
- Wesley S. Lybrand, 20th Regiment, SC Infantry
- John D. Lybrand, born 1841, He served with Company A 9th Regiment, Arkansas infantry during Civil War. Received medical discharge November 14, 1961 at Columbus, KY.
- *John Noah Lybrand, Born September 20, 1836 - Died December 1, 1862 in Civil War

* Points out those Lybrand's that died in the Civil War.

One cute story that was passed down to me by Jack Lybrand was that Wesley Allen and his wife were sitting on their front porch. Wesley Allen was smoking a pipe and somehow it got turned over in his mouth and the burning content fell in his lap and burnt though his pants. He got up slapping and slapping his pants trying to put it out. His wife told everyone that he even burned his "tally wacker."

<h1 style="text-align:center">(G.W.) George Washington Lybrand</h1>

November 19, 1848-June 5, 1935

The following is a picture of George Washington Lybrand and his wife Sara Jane Jackson Lybrand. This picture was provided by Jack Lybrand, his grandson. His father was Fred C. Lybrand, George Washington's and Sara Jane's son.

The following is a picture I took of George Washington Lybrand's and Sara Jane Lybrand's tombstone. They are buried in the New Holland Cemetery near Wesley Allen Lybrand's Tombstone.

Daddy told me that his granddaddy, who was called GW, raised large hoofed horses used to pull heavy loads and he remembered how beautiful they were. He also told me that he would buy almost anything that he thought he could buy and resell at a profit. I have an old deed with his signature on it. I have copied it and placed it below.

I have in my possession three old deeds that were among Daddy' s possessions.

The first deed is from G.W. Lybrand to Fred C. Lybrand for $100.00 conveying one acre by church land and property belonging to G.W. Lybrand. It is dated January 14, 1914. It was signed G.W. Lybrand and Jane Lybrand renounced her dower. As you probably know by now, Fred C. Lybrand was George Washington's son.

The second deed is from G.W. Lybrand to J.S. Lybrand for $62.00 conveying lots 13 & 14 in New Holland. It is dated October 24, 1919. It was signed by G.W. Lybrand and Jane Lybrand renounced her dower. G.W. Lybrand's signature was witnessed by Mrs. Mamie Lybrand. Of course, J.S. Lybrand was John Samuel Lybrand, my grandfather.

WITNESS _my_ Hand_ and Seal_, this _24_ day of _Oct_ in the year of our Lord one thousand nine hundred and _Nineteen_ and in the one hundred and _44_ year of the Sovereignty and Independence of the United States of America.

SIGNED, SEALED AND DELIVERED
IN THE PRESENCE OF

_M C Hutto_       _G. M. Lybrand_ (L. S.)

_Mrs Mannie Lybrand_ (L. S.)

The third deed is from G.W. Lybrand to C. W. Jackson with no monetary value placed on the deed. It was for one quarter of an acre in the midst of property belonging to G. W. Lybrand. It was dated February 3, 1910. It was signed by G.W. Lybrand and Sarah Jane Lybrand renounced her dower. I am not sure who C.W. Jackson was. It is my guess that he was a relative of Jane Lybrand.

For many years in America a married woman was protected by law from her husband selling property without his wife knowing about the sale and leaving his wife penniless. This right was called her "Dower Right." Therefore, a man could not sell any property unless his wife released her "Dower Right."

At a closing she had to be taken aside and out of the presence of her husband and made sure she understood her rights and was not being forced to sign her dower rights away. This was done away with a good many years ago while I was still in real estate. It was always interesting to see the attorney take the wife out of the room during a closing to have her sign her dower right away so property could be sold.

The following is how the dower was renounced on the deed to J.S. Lybrand mentioned above. Note that Jane Lybrand signed this dower release.

THE STATE OF SOUTH CAROLINA, Aiken County.

RENUNCIATION OF DOWER.

I, C. C. Fox, NKSC do hereby certify unto all whom it may concern, that Mrs. Jane Lybrand the wife of the within named J. S. Lybrand did this day appear before me, and upon being privately and separately examined by me, did declare that she does freely, voluntarily, and without any compulsion, dread or fear of any person or persons whomsoever renounce, release and forever relinquish unto the within named J. S. Lybrand his Heirs and Assigns, all her interest and estate, and also all her right and claim of dower, of, in or to all and singular, the premises within mentioned and released.

Given under my Hand and Seal, this 24 day of Oct. Anno Domini 1919.

C. C. Fox (SEAL.) NKSC

Jane Lybrand

At the time of signing of the deed from George Washington Lybrand to John Samuel Lybrand, George Washington was 70 years old. Jane, his wife was 63 years old, John Samuel was 47 years old and Mamie was 41 years old.

The following is a letter I got from Frances Tyler, George Washington's granddaughter. Her father was Fred Clay Lybrand,

George Washington's son. I have copied it just as she has written it. I like recording information I got like this because it reveals something about the personality of those that have sent me material on the Lybrand clan. Her address was Wagener, SC.

*"May 8, 2012*
*Dear Sam,*

*I was surprised to hear from you, but happy. I remember you and Tommy when you would come to New Holland to visit your grandmother.*

*I'm afraid I can't add much to what you have.*

*What I remember about George Washington was that he was heavy and could hardly get around. He chewed tobacco and it was always dribbling on his white shirt After his children were gone and he was alone he went to Wagener with his daughter Bessie and husband Dr. John Hallman Brodie and lived with them until he died.*

*I remember he would come to New Holland and spend a few days with us on the farm He would want to go into the field where daddy and the boys were working, and I would go with him and carry a box (I was about 8). He would walk a short distance and say, "baby bring the box" and he would sit down and rest. This was repeated until we got back to the house.*

*I was 12 when he died and his funeral was held at the old home place in the drive way which was lined with hedges on both sides. The old home place was on the right from your grandmother's house to the cemetery. The house has been torn down. I don't have any pictures.*

*Your grandfather, John Samuel, died the year I was born. (I'm 88.) so I don't know much about him I remember Aunt Mamie saying that when the children were young, they would be sitting together talking about the past and Sue would say where was I, daddy? (She wasn't born yet.) He would say, "You were under the bed", and it would always satisfy her.*

*LeMyra plans to send you a group of pictures with your Grandfather in it. I've heard it said that Uncle Sammy would wake Aunt Mamie up at night and tell her he was so hungry. She would get up and cook something/or him*

*Your father being 20 years older than me I don't know about his early years. He did teach at New Holland. The school house still stands, but not used as a school. Times were bad back in these days. I remember your mother and father visiting his mother on Sunday and as they got ready to leave Jennie said to Harvey, "Your Mother needs some change to mail some letters" He reached in his pocket and gave here some change. Letters, postage was only 2 or 3 cents back then, but as I said times were hard.*

*I remember your grandmother really well. We lived about ½ mile from her past the cemetery. I went to her house nearly every Sunday afternoon to play with Frances Hydrick. She was Methodist. The church was next door. It is now closed. Sue played the Piano at the church for services.*

*Aunt Mamie was a very sweet person. She was a Clayton from around the Camp Long Area. I know she had family but I didn't know them.*

*Sue didn't ' t like to be by herself at night. I spent many nights with her when she was alone. When I was at her house and it would rain and thunder and lightning Sue would have us lie across the bed and get our feet off the floor.*

*Her house was always neat, as was her yard. She owned probably 5 or 6 acres of land. She always had a good garden. She had a peach orchard behind the house also pecan trees. She had a cow and chickens. Fred Hydrick gave her a pig each year to help out. She raised Frances after Thelma Died.*

*I don't remember seeing Aunt Mamie wear anything colorful. It was always white with a black print or a dark color. I think it's wonderful that you are putting this together for your children and grandchildren. Sorry, I'm afraid I'm not much help.*

*Hope you can read this scratching. I don't see too well. I live by myself (My husband passed away 5 years ago.) We had been married 63 years. I have 2 children, LeMyra 66 and Charlie 62 - 3 grandsons, 40 - 32 - 30.*

*My husband and I owned and operated a grocery store (His grandmother started it.) I worked in it for 40 years. I was 72 when I retired. My husband was 75.*

*Well, enough about me.*

*Sorry I didn't have any pictures. Good luck in putting it all together. So good to hear from you.*

*Love and Best Wishes From your old Cousin Francis Lybrand Tyler"*

(What a wonderful letter and she said she did not have anything to say. Boy, did she tell it all!)

LeMyra, (Whose mother wrote the above letter to me and who I have mentioned before), writes for the **Wagener Monthly**. After I talked to her and ask for information about what she knew about the Lybrand's she wrote an article about some stories her mother told her. The following is a portion of this article. Note that she called my grandmother Mame instead of Mamie as I call her and her mother called her. (Wednesday, May 30, 2012 edition - Where article came from.)

*''Aunt Mame lived across the road from New Holland Baptist Church. Mama recalls that Aunt Mame always had a garden and fruit trees and her house was always spotless. Mama also said that Aunt Mame was very neat and always wore dresses with a black background.*

*I questioned Mama about this, and she told me that all those many years ago that many women wore black because their husbands were dead.*

*Several days after I spoke with Sam Lybrand, I told Mama that we were riding to New Holland Cemetery. I jokingly said that I had a few questions for some of the Lybrand relatives buried there.*

*My great-great grandfather Wesley Allen Lybrand and great-great mother Sarah Elizabeth Lybrand and my great-grandfather George Washington Lybrand are all buried at the New Holland cemetery. Uncle Sammy, Aunt Mame and a lot of other Lybrand uncles, aunts and cousins are buried there, too.*

*After arriving at the cemetery, Mama and I got out of the car and began to walk through the cemetery reading the inscriptions on the graves and discussing how each one was related to us. We came to great-grandpa George's brother, Noah Webster Lybrand's grave; he died from being bitten by a rabid dog.*

*George W. and Jane had six other children besides Sammy and Fred: Aunt Corrie, of whom I often speak, was the oldest girl. I probably knew her better than any of Pa Fred's siblings.*

*When Grandmama Leila Lybrand was alive, Sunday afternoon was a time to ride to New Holland. Almost always, we would eventually visit with Aunt Corrie who lived on highway 39 between Oak Grove and New*

*Holland. I remember Aunt Corrie always laughing about most everything. She never let life get her down.*

*Her youngest daughter Faye was the age of Mama, and Mama had told me many tales about Faye and herself. One of my favorites is just after Faye's daughter Gloria Jean was born. She was at Aunt Corries's house and Eugene Buckingham, more affectionately known as "Punk", said, "Ma'ah you better go in there and see about the baby; Faye is dragging her around like a sack of peas."*

*Also, when we were at the cemetery, Mama told me a tale about her daddy and Cousin Annie Boatwright Johnson's husband Claude. Pa Fred and Claude were fishing from a boat in the river.*

*It seems that Claude had taken off his hat and placed it in the bottom of the boat behind him. Pa Fred told Claude to get his hat, as it was getting water in il Claude began to retrieve his hat and in doing so he also began to moan ... ooh. ooh, ooh, then louder oooh, oooh, all the while bumping his hat from one hand to the other. Well, a snake had fallen from a tree into the boat, and Pa Fred had managed to slip the snake into Claude's hat; I can just imagine the Jun Pa Fred had with that stunt. Mama went on to say that Pa Fred came home and told Grandmama Leila what he had done.*

*After they had a good laugh, Grandmama asked, "What happened to Claude's hat?" Pa Fred replied that the last time he had seen it, it was spinning down the river."*

I got an email from James Lybrand, George Washington's grandson. His father was Allen. He sent me picture of John Samuel and Mamie's house, in an updated condition, and a picture of the Methodist Church he is sure Wesley Allen, George Washington and John Samuel's families all went to. He related that George Washington gave the land and paid for the material to build this old church which is now not in regular use. He also sent me a picture of his father, Allen, and his mother, Cora Toole Lybrand, which I have included along with the picture of John Samuel's home place and the Methodist Church.

He also related that his grandfather, George Washington, worked with timber logging and would raft logs down the Edisto River to the mills. He stated that his father, Allen was born in 1884 and was 84 years old when he died. He also related that his father was a farmer.

**John Samuel Lybrand - May 3, 1872 - November 28, 1924**

The following is a picture taken in the late 1800s of John Samuel Lybrand and his bride, Mamie Louise Clayton Lybrand. These two pictures were gratefully provided by Marcia Hydrick Foreman. She is the great granddaughter of John Samuel and Mamie Louise. Her father is Ray Hydrick and his mother was Thelma, John Samuel's and Mamie Louise's oldest child. These pictures were taken in Augusta, GA. My father often talked about his father doing most of his selling and business in Augusta.

This is the tombstone of John Samuel Lybrand and Mamie
Louise Lybrand in the New Holland, SC cemetery

This is a picture of John Samuel's and Mamie Louise's house in New Holland, SC. This picture was taken in 2012 by Jimmy Lybrand, one of George Washington's grandsons. He lives in Salley, SC, not far from the New Holland area. As stated before, he also has very graciously provided several other pictures and information about the Lybrand clan.

When I visited Granny's house in the late 1930s and early 1940s this was a working farm and the house was unpainted and looked old, at least it looked that way to a young child at the time. Now it is nicely fixed up and looks like any modern home.

This is the home place of Sammie and Mamie Lybrand in New Holland
Your grandfather and grandmother

In one of Marcia Hydrick Foreman's stories she described the location of this old house in a story about the house her father, Ray, lived in as a youth. This brings to light something about former times.

*"My dad grew up on a farm in New Holland, SC. He lived in a house built before the Civil War by Uncle Elmore Jones who had 365 acres of land in New Holland. Uncle Elmore was a Confederate soldier during the War Between the Sates. He and his brother walked all the way back home from*

*Virginia after the war ended. His brother died on the way home but Uncle Elmore made it all the way back. The farm house had a great porch on the side of it with a water spigot with a dipper and a wooden bowl full of the best cold water in South Carolina. There is a smoke house and a barn and a chicken coop and a pig sty on the farm. The house has a kitchen, a dining room, a master bedroom, one bathroom, a parlor, and a guest bedroom and a nice screened-in front porch. There is an outhouse in the yard, to use until the new bathroom was added on the old house. I can still remember my Papa, Fred Q. Hydrick, sitting on the porch waiting on us to come visit him. Daddy would always sit outside on the porch and talk to his dad while Mother and I would go inside and talk to Azalea. I used to love to go visit them. My dad and my Papa put the tin roof on the old house.*

*Down the dirt road from the farm, you can turn left on the paved road and it will take you to New Holland. My great grandfather, John Samuel Lybrand, had a general store there. He and my granny, Mamie Lybrand, lived in the big white house that sat across the street from the general store. They lived next door to the Methodist Church. Across the street from their house was the Baptist Church and the New Holland graveyard where my mother is buried.*

*If you turn right from the farm, and drive down the dirt road you will find Elmore Jones' graveyard, He married Frances Hydrick."*

Marcia's story fills in a lot of blanks in telling where the Methodist Church was and where John Samuel's general store was located. (I am thankful to Marcia for putting her story about her father titled "The Ray Philip Hydricks of Aiken, SC." on the internet.)

All during all my life time I have heard about Thelma, Daddy's oldest sister, but had no idea what she looked like and did not know much about her. But thanks to Cousin Marcia Hydrick Foreman, I now have a copy of Thelma's picture taken not long before she died. I believe the young child in the picture is her daughter, Frances, who I knew very well and spent time with as a young boy.

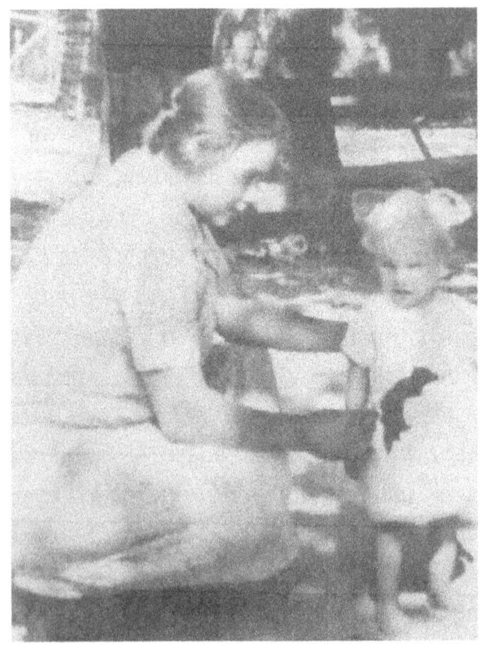

Pictured below are Thelma's sons, Kenny and Rhett and Marcia's father, Ray. Daddy's sister, Sue, is also pictured. Kenny and Rhett have already died. Ray is still living and is over 90 years old in 2012.

I put Thelma's sons in this book because I had something to do with them coming up. As related in my earlier story, I went to New York with The Citadel band, which I was a member of, to play before the New York Yankee's baseball game. While I was up there, Rhett came and got me and took me to his house for a meal and to spend some time with his wife and daughter. I'll always remember going into this huge city with all its roads and bridges after being raised on Edisto with all it creeks and wide open areas of marsh grass where there was only one main road across the whole of Edisto Island. I was in awe at this amazing mass of people going here and there and Cousin Rhett knowing where to go.

Kenny spent one winter with us on Edisto helping Daddy build the dining room on the Ocean Villa he just bought to expand his business. I was told that Kenny, even though he was a professional carpenter, had a hard time coping with life because during the Second World War he was in one of those long Japanese marches in the Philippines and almost died. He really never got over this and after the war led a very subdued life. His brother Rhett looked after him and even built a house for him on a lake in the New Holland, Wagener area.

Ray owned a kitchen appliance store in Aiken, SC and I remember going there as a child when we visited Aiken. He and his wife Mary often came to Edisto to visit during Lybrand family gatherings. A few years ago, Joyce and I went to Aiken to Ray's 90th birthday celebration.

Since I am telling about Thelma, I have included a picture of her tombstone. In this Lybrand family plot where John Samuel and Mamie Louise are buried, Thelma's baby that died at birth, Rhett, Kenny and Ray's wife Mary are also buried.

Over the course of this book I have given you a lot of material about John Samuel Lybrand, my grandfather on Daddy's side. He sounded like a busy and productive man during his life time. He farmed and ran a general merchandise store. One thing that I like is that I have his Bible with his name written in the front of it. As you will see from the sermon given at my father's funeral, he was also a religious man who believed strongly in the standards of behavior found in the Bible.

# Harvie Samuel Lybrand - August 2, 1904 - November 25, 1997

The following are pictures of my father and mother. The loneliest day of my life was when my mother died. She just did things for me and told me she loved me over and over again, no matter what the circumstances were and whatever I had done. As long as you have a mother cherish her until the day she dies and speak kindly of her after she dies.

My father was there for me always and came to my rescue whenever I needed him. He constantly advised me of the way I should go. He lived a long and productive life and seemed to enjoy living and accomplishing things. Golf was his passion and he played until he was in his early nineties.

My father and mother are buried in the graveyard of The Presbyterian Church on Edisto Island. He was a Ruling Elder there for 30 years and my mother often sang solos during church services. I joined this church at about age 13. Most of my childhood activities were through this church.

At the right, is my father's obituary as it appeared in the Charleston News and Courier. He spent the last year of his life in the Presbyterian Home in Summerville, SC.

CHARLESTON
NEWS & COURIER

## Harvie Lybrand

EDISTO BEACH — Harvie S. Lybrand, 93, first mayor of Edisto Beach, died Tuesday in a Summerville nursing home. The funeral will be at 11 a.m. Saturday in The Presbyterian Church on Edisto Island. Burial, directed by Dyal Funeral Home of Summerville, will be in the church cemetery.

Mr. Lybrand was born in New Holland, a son of John S. Lybrand and Mamie Clayton Lybrand. He was a graduate of New Holland High School and Wofford College. He was a former operator of the Ocean Villa bed and breakfast. He was a member of the Lions Club and The Presbyterian Church on Edisto Island.

Surviving are his wife, Evelyn M. Lybrand; two sons, Sam Lybrand of Columbia and David L. Lybrand of Edisto Island; 13 grandchildren; and 12 great-grandchildren.

These are some of my
favorite pictures of
my mother.

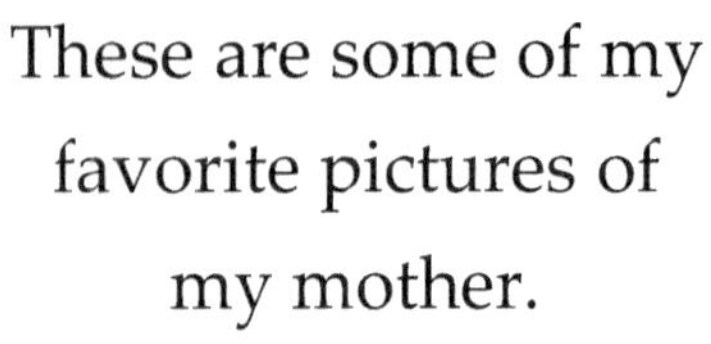

This copy of the inside of a Bible that Mother gave to Daddy the year after they were married should stand alone. It shows that our family was a Christ believing family at its beginning. Praise be the holy name of Jesus Christ!

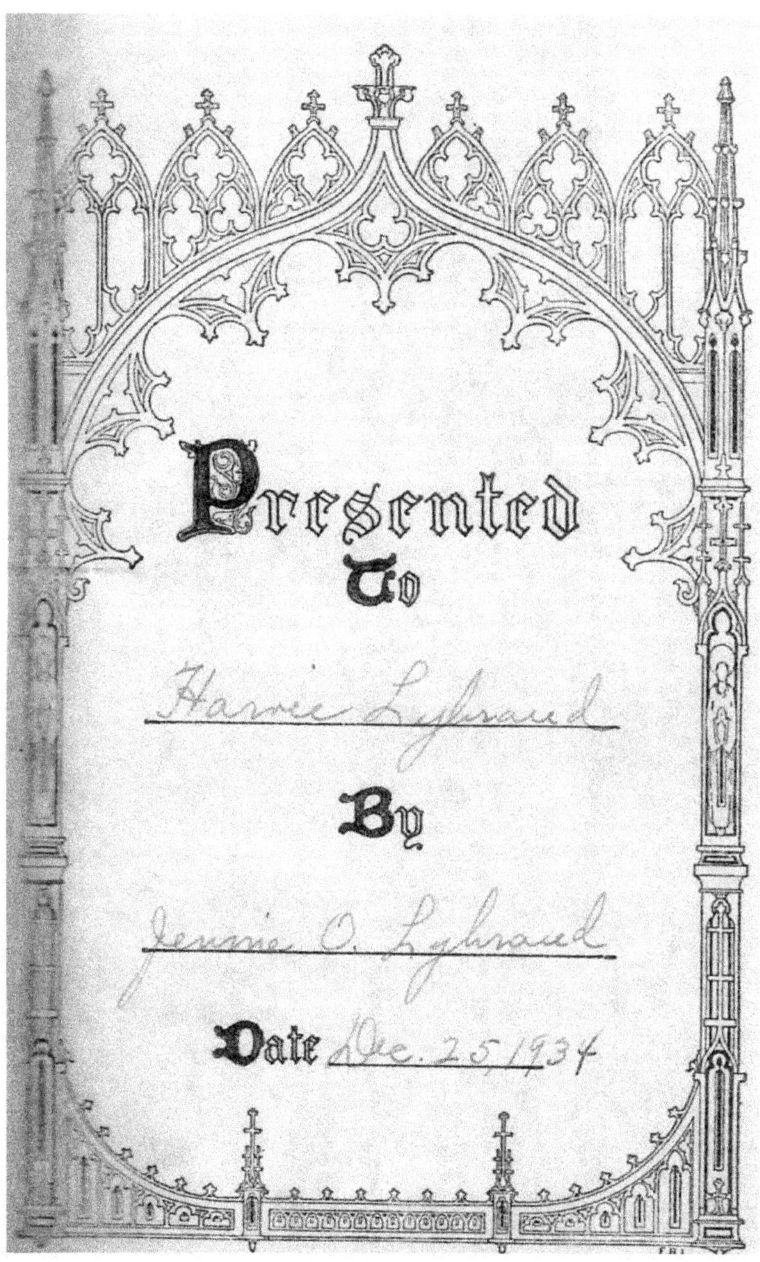

This is one of the best pictures I have of my Daddy. I am not sure when it was taken and who the child is sitting in his lap being shown pictures to or being read to.

 My older brother, Thomas Harvie Lybrand, died an untimely death. He is also buried in The Presbyterian Church on Edisto Island, SC. Here is a picture of his tombstone and a couple of family pictures.

On May 29, 1975 The Press and Standard Newspaper out of Walterboro, SC published the following article.

## "Mayor A Long-Time Beach Resident"

*"A resident of Edisto Beach since 1947, Harvey Lybrand has been mayor of the town since its incorporation in 1970.*

*Although the Lybrand's move to the beach was made for health reasons, they liked the beach and decided to live there permanently, he said.*

*While living in Aiken, one of their three sons contracted a nasal infection, and a doctor recommended that they move to the beach for a healthier climate. The infection cleared up immediately, Lybrand said, and the family enjoyed beach living so much that they stayed.*

*"I was traveling with a publishing company then and I got tired of it," Lybrand said, "I wanted to be with my family more. One week I made up my mind to quit and stay here. My hair almost went gray with the decision, but I took a chance and I've never regretted it."*

*He bought property on the beach and rented rooms and cottages to visitors, and also operated a tearoom. As evidence of the beach's growth since then, a piece of property sold then for $600 would now bring $25,000. Lybrand said.*

*The population and number of rental houses have grown relatively slowly since then. Lybrand accounts for the lack of any large development on the beach to the fact that "the original owners of Edisto didn't tell anybody about it."*

*"In a way I'm glad it grew." he said. "You can't stop what we call progress." With more houses being built. Edisto became much more of a year-round resort, he said.*

*Lybrand echoed the opinion of other residents when he said. "This is purely a family beach - there's nothing to do but play in the surf or go to the pavilion."*

*As mayor, Lybrand says he is "delighted to be in Colleton County." The town is now planning a city-county complex with cost shared by Colleton County and Edisto Beach, to include an office for the Town Clerk, a room for the four-member Town Council to meet, and headquarters for the resident deputy and the volunteer fire department."*

Pictures of my father and mother that went along with this write up

**First a filler picture taken in our Aiken backyard**

The Press and Standard, Thursday, May 29, 1975

Edisto Beach Mayor Harvey Lybrand

# Mayor A Long-Time Beach Resident

Mrs. Jennie Lybrand Enjoys Greenhouse Plants

The following eulogy was given by Rev. Stephen Keeler on the occasion of Daddy's death. It is a good description of what kind of man he was and what people through of him.

"A Homily
By: Rev. Stephen Keeler (Mother and Daddy's favorite
Preacher)
In loving Memory of Harvie Lybrand
November 29, 1997"
(He died November 25, 1997)

"We come here today to worship God and to thank him as family and friends for the life of Harvie Lybrand. As I look back on the life of Harvie Lybrand, I believe the following words of the New Testament describe him as a man, a father, grandfather and friend.

*"(One) should be temperate, worthy of respect, self-controlled, and sound in faith, in love and endurance."* (Titus 2:2)

Life is a challenge for all of us as I am sure it was a challenge for Harvie Lybrand One does not marry, raise a family, make a living, and face the rising sun without challenges. In life, there are days of opportunity and we often rejoice when things go smoothly. There are also days when things get turned upside down. In moments of confusion, our response may be uneven. We do not always think or react in the context of moderation, respectability, self-control, or faith because we may be upset, angry- discouraged ... even brokenhearted. And yet, life is a wonderful mystery where ebb and flow, joy and tragedy introduce us to the providence of God, the grace of Jesus Christ and the benevolent power of the Holy Spirit

Harvie Lybrand understood, I believe, the wisdom of the Scriptures that tell us that there is a season for everything. There is a time to be born and a time to die, a time to weep and a time to laugh, a time to mourn and a time to dance. As the seasons come and go, we are called to demonstrate in our lives moderation, respectability, discipline, and faith. These attributes are punctuated by our willingness to love and be loved, and the resolve to experience and endure the mystery of life with a confident and resilient spirit. This, for me, describes the man we knew as Harvie Lybrand.

It was in 1982, having graduated from seminary and receiving the call to the Edisto church, that I had the privilege of getting to know Harvie and his gracious family. Over the years I learned of his early career traveling from one school district to another introducing educators to the best text books available. I also learned of his tenure as a leader in public education, of the exodus to Edisto Beach in order to provide a healthy environment for his family, of his success as a business man and the many weeks, months, and years that the Lybrand's served visitors and guests and made many a friend on the beach of a southern, sea barrier island. When one lives on an island that is nearly twelve miles long and eight miles wide, connected to the mainland by a drawbridge, it is important to live moderately and make good friends.

Looking back, Harvie Lybrand understood the boundaries of life except for maybe, one particular area, and that was, of course, the fame and sport of golf. In my occasional exploits on the golf course with friends, I still tell the story of having played years ago with an eighty plus year old man who hit every shot from tee to green right down the middle of the fairway. His chipping around the green was spectacular and his success. Whereas I always fell prey to the adrenalin at Fairfield to pull out the driver and go for it, usually landing in the water or an oasis of trees, almost out of bounds, Harvie was always patient. He understood the importance of selecting the right club and of applying just the right tempo in his swing. From Harvie I learned the important lesson: It is not how you start the race, but how you finish it. In six years plus of competition on the golf course, I was bigger, stronger, and I thought sometimes wiser than Harvie Lybrand. And yet, not once was I ever victorious in head-to-head competition. I think it often amused him.

In a more serious side, Harvie Lybrand was a man who people respected for his quiet demeanor, keen insight, and gentle Spirit. Harvie helped to guide this congregation through reunion with northern Presbyterians and supported the programs that nurtured the children and young families of this parish. In session meeting, he always spoke as an elder who emulated the practical spirituality of the Christian prayer: Lord may you grant us the courage to change the things we can, the peace to accept the things we cannot change, and the wisdom to know the difference.

In an age where many people push the envelope on self-control, Harvie Lybrand understood how to share his feelings, thoughts, and emotions in constructive ways that were careful not to offend. In all the personal connection and important people he knew, I never saw Harvie Lybrand as an arrogant or conceited man. Instead, he was a secure and confident man.

Harvie Lybrand was also a man who was - as the Bible says - sound in faith. Was he a saint? Probably not. If there is anything we all share - whether we like to admit it or not - it is our human brokenness. But Harvie was faithful ... as a church- goer, as a man knowledgeable of the Scripture, and as a human being who found it imperative to live out the gospel in the common experience of everyday life. Harvie loved God and his neighbor in a quiet distinct way.

Now a brief word about love and endurance. Harvie Lybrand was a man who loved his family. He was devoted to them and deeply proud of all their accomplishments. He lived the life of a faithful husband, loving father and grandfather.

The word endurance speaks to itself. Harvie Lybrand lived a long life of ninety plus years. Can you imagine the changes, the transformation, this man experienced? When one reads over the Bible and studies the lives of those who experienced long, vibrant pilgrimages, it seems that they were the people who understood three important lessons: First, life is a complex mystery that is often beyond human understanding. Somewhere you have to gain the insight that you are not in control, but God is. Second, the Lord God is at both the beginning and the end of life, one had better meet him somewhere in between, and third, living in the grace of Jesus Christ giving one the confidence and the Christian hope to face the changes and transition of today and tomorrow with a certain sense of anticipation and excitement.

Finally, the Scriptures teach that, in Christ, we are to live moderate, morally upright, self-controlled, and faithful lives. In addition, we are to love others as we are loved and to do so with a confident, quiet hope and knowing when the end of life is coming. There things - to me - describe the life and Christian witness of Harvie Lybrand. Thanks be to God. Amen."

## George Samuel Lybrand Born April 3, 1937 in Aiken, SC

The following is the picture of me that I want to be remembered by. My feather hat keeps me cool in the summer while I go fishing or walk on the beach. When I walk on the beach with my feather hat on, I get stopped several times and asked what the significance of the hat is. I tell them it is just a collection of feathers I have collected on the beach and feathers my children and grandchildren have given me. One was brought to me from Maine by one of Joyce's grandsons.

This picture was taken on our dock next to our fish cleaning table. Our house is seen in the background.

This picture was taken of me in our camellia garden. Currently I have over 100 varieties of camellias in this garden which requires a good bit of my time keeping it clean. I have some in the ground and some in containers as you see in the background. The garden has many little statuaries of all types for the children to enjoy. The camellia pictured below is named Anticipation.

This next picture is of Joyce and me in our vegetable garden standing among our okra plants. We have something growing year-round and many of our meals come from this garden. You can see a fence in the background. It is an eight-foot-high welded wire fence to keep the deer and rabbits out.

I will be cremated. Half my ashes will be placed in the grave beside my first wife Ida who is buried in the Boone Hill United Methodist Church graveyard in Knightsville, SC. She is buried in a Myers family plot next to the graves of her mother and father. The other half of my ashes will be placed beside my second wife Joyce. She will be buried in the graveyard of The Presbyterian Church on Edisto Island, SC. If I die before she does, I have requested that my ashes be kept and buried with her upon her death and burial. I consider Edisto Island as home and want a part of me to always be on Edisto Island. Both ladies have given me meaning and joy in my life. Ida gave me three fine children and Joyce has been a great companion in my older age. Here is a picture of the tombstone where Ida is buried and where my name is already placed with my date of birth.

Since I have a picture of my father's and mother's tombstone, I thought it only proper for me to put a picture of my children's grandparent's tombstone on my wife's side in this book. I am also including a couple of pictures of them. If my children want to trace this side of the family this will be a good start.

194

Here is a picture of the Lady I married on December 23, 1959,
Ida Margaret Myers.

Here is a copy of our wedding announcement and a picture of us going on our honeymoon. I was re sed in my blue U.S. Coast Guard Uniform. I had just graduated and comm1ss 1oned as an office on December 20, 1959

## Ida Margaret Myers Becomes Bride Of George S. Lybrand

SUMMERVILLE (Special) — Miss Ida Margaret Myers, a daughter of Mr. and Mrs. James Arnold Myers of Summerville, and Mr. George Samuel Lybrand, a son of Mr. and Mrs. Harvie Samuel Lybrand of Edisto Beach, were married Wednesday at Knightsville Methodist Church. The Rev. Joseph E. Tysinger officiated.

Given in marriage by her father, the bride wore a waltz-length gown of rose-point lace and tulle over satin fashioned with a scooped neckline adorned with pearls and sequins. The bouffant skirt had panels of tulle with appliques of lace. Her shoulder-length three-tiered veil of French silk illusion was held in place with a tiarra of seed pearls. She carried a cascade bouquet of feathered carnations and stephanotis centered with an orchid.

Miss Barbara Alice Myers of Bartow, Fla., and Summerville was maid of honor for her sister. She wore a waltz-length gown of red lace over matching taffeta that featured a red butterfly bow at the back. She carried a cascade bouquet of white carnations.

Bridesmaids were Miss Lottle Hanson Cummings of Summerville and Miss Mary Geneva Harley of Dorchester, a cousin of the bride. They carried cascade bouquets of white carnations also and wore gowns that matched that of Miss Myer's.

The bridegroom's father acted as best man. Ushers were Mr. David Ladson Lybrand a brother of the bridegroom, and Mr. Michael Harley Pate of Dorchester, a cousin of the bride.

Following the ceremony a reception was held in the social hall of the church. After a wedding trip in the Caribbean the couple will reside in San Juan, Puerto Rico.

The bride was graduated from Summerville High School and the Medical College of South Carolina School of Nursing.

The bridegroom was graduated from St. Paul's High School and from The Citadel and holds a commission as an ensign in the U.S. Coast Guard.

Here is a picture of Ida's and my three children, their spouses and some of their children. Picture taken in July of 2012

Top left: My oldest, Jimmy and his wife Melinda

Bottom left: Matt, Amy's husband; Amy, Robert and Anne. Amy is our second child.

Bottom right: John Daniel, Liz, John's wife; and Sarah and John, John is our youngest child.

My children told me to put that they all had just been in the creek.

Missing are Jim's Laken and Sam

A few more family pictures:

Four generations

My Daddy, Me, Jimmy and Jimmy's son Sam

Ida's Mother, Ida, Jimmy and Jimmy's son Sam

Random pictures of my family

I have led an interesting life. I went to a two room school house in grammar school and was the only one in the seventh grade. We lived on Edisto Beach and for the first several years we were one of only three families that lived on the beach during the winter. Behind my house I had 500 acres to explore all to myself. I also had the only sailboat on Big Bay Creek. One year I drove the school bus in high school. In high school I took Agriculture which I still use to this day, I was elected to represent the High School at Boy's State and I was a member of a small dance band playing the drums called the "Hollywood Ramblers." Our theme song was the "Muskrat Ramblers." After High School I had the privilege of attending and graduating from The Citadel, the Military College of South Carolina, one of the nation's top USA colleges. While at The Citadel I was a member of the Bagpipe Corp playing the Scott Drum. During college I marched in the President Eisenhower Inaugural Parade and played, for a week, at New York Yankee stadium the last time the Yankees played the Braves before they moved to Atlanta, GA. I also helped start the first sailing team at The Citadel. After college I became an officer in the U.S. Coast Guard and served in Puerto Rico and Miami, Florida. Between OCS and my first assignment I got married and Jimmy came along shortly thereafter. In the Coast Guard I had a lot of responsibility and got to see some unique parts of the world. After the Coast Guard I spent eight years in industry working myself up from an expediter to a material manager. My first job out of the service was at Utica Tool in Orangeburg, SC. During our stay in Orangeburg, Ida and I also had two more children, Amy and John. Since I moved four times in industry, I decided to settle down and in 1970 and went into full time residential real estate sales and just retired in 2011. I spent 30 years selling in Columbia, SC and 11 years selling on Edisto Island, SC. During all this I became a Deacon for two terms and a Ruling Elder for four terms in the Presbyterian Church. In 1985 I was the spark God used to establish a new Presbyterian Church that now has over 1000 members (The St. Andrews Presbyterian Church - PCA). In 1988 I had a serious heart by-pass. In 1993 Ida came down with lupus and seven years later in 2000 died of the disease. In late 2000 I moved back to Edisto and married Joyce. In 2004 I was told I was going to die of pancreatic cancer. It is obvious that the doctor was wrong because it is seven years later and I am still here. I retired from real estate sales in 2011. Therefore, I have had a varied and interesting life.

**Here is summary of where I have lived and a few events:**

| | |
|---|---|
| April 3, 1937 | Born in Aiken County Hospital |
| 1937-1947 | Lived in Aiken, SC |
| 1942-1947 | Spent the summers on Edisto Beach |
| Fall of 1947 | The family moved to Edisto full time. |
| 1947-1950 | Went to the Edisto Island Grammar School |
| 1950-1955 | Went to St. Paul's High in Hollywood, SC |
| Summer of 1954 | Attended Boys State in Columbia, SC 1947- |
| 1959 | Lived on Edisto Beach, SC |
| 1955-1959 | Attended the Citadel & Graduated |
| Aug. - Dec. 1959 | Attended Coast Guard OCS and Commissioned as Ensign after completing OCS (Office Candidate School) in December of 1959. |

| | |
|---|---|
| Dec. 23, 1959 | Married Ida Margaret Myers |
| 1960-1961 | Stationed in San Juan, Puerto Rico in Coast Guard |
| October 11, 1960 | Jimmy was born in San Juan, Puerto Rico Stationed in |
| 1961-1962 | Miami, Florida in Coast Guard Worked at Utica Tool |
| 1962-1966 | in Orangeburg, SC |
| 1963 | Amy was born in Orangeburg, SC |
| 1965 | John was born in Orangeburg, SC |
| 1966-1969 | Worked at General Electric in Hendersonville, NC |
| 1969 | Worked at Argus and Monroe Calculator in |
| 1970-2000 | Columbia Worked in Real Estate in Columbia, SC |
| 1972 | Built house at 600 Whitefalls Drive in Coldstream in Irmo, SC |
| 1985 | God used me as the spark that begin the St. Andrews Presbyterian Church in Irmo, SC |
| 1988 | Had serious heart by-pass - Blue Cross insurance canceled my health insurance because of the heart by-pass. They told me I had now used my insurance. |

| 1993-2000 | Ida was sick with Lupus in Columbia, SC |
| 1995 | Sold house in Coldstream and moved into apartment because of Ida's illness |
| 1996 | Went broke and Ida was put in nursing home |
| 1996 | Moved in with my son Jimmy in Pelion, SC |
| 1997 -2000 | Bought Mobile Home in Pelion, SC next door to my son Jimmy and lived there until I moved back to Edisto |
| March 2000 | Ida died |
| November 2000 | Moved back to Edisto and Married Joyce Hills Abrams |
| 2001-2011 | Worked at Edisto Realty |
| August 2004 | Was told I was going to die of pancreatic cancer. (God was not ready for me and I am still living.) |
| September 2004 | Was operated on to remove cancerous tumor from my pancreas. |
| Nov. 2004-April 2005 | Received Chemotherapy to prevent cancer from coming back. |
| April 2011 | Retired from Real Estate after 41 years |
| April 2011 | Started writing this book. |
| June 2012 | The doctors told me not to come back - They said that if the cancer was going to come back it would have come back by now. Praise the good Lord! |

Before I sum it all up here is a picture taken for our church directory of Joyce and me. She has brought great joy and happiness to me since the fall of 2000. She and I went to school together in grammar and high school and dated a few times during college. When Ida died, I came back home and married her and moved back to Edisto. We currently live in a house she inherited after her first husband died. We both like the creeks and we both like to garden. With our combined seven children, 15 grandchildren and one great-grandchild our lives are full and there is something going on constantly.

Again, all I can say is that the Lybrand clan is an interesting bunch. My greatest desire is that all my children and grandchildren will begin keep a record of what experiences they have as they go through life and write them all down for their descendants. Then in years to come there will be a true record of what the Sam Lybrand's did and accomplished during their lives.

God bless you all, every one of you.

Granddaddy Sam

### Gloria Patri

*Glory be to the Father, and to the Son, and to the Holy Ghost: As it was in the beginning, is now, is now, and ever shall be, world without end. Amen, Amen.*

Mother & Granny

Me

Mother on left on beach

Me

Ida

# Remembering

1932                                                            1982

Please join our family
on the joyous occasion
of the Fiftieth Anniversary
of the marriage of
Jennie Owens and Harvie Lybrand
on Sunday, the twenty-seventh of June
from four to six o'clock
at their home
Edisto Beach, South Carolina

No gifts please

50th Wedding Anniversary
Aunt Bessie, Mother, Aunt Ruby, Uncle George and Daddy

# Remembering

Me

David

Ida & Mother

Harvie & Jennie

**What a life I have lived so far! What possibly can top what has already gone past in what years God has ordained for me to live.**

*But you are a chosen race, a royal priesthood, a holy nation, a people for God's own possession, that you may proclaim the excellencies of Him who had called you out of darkness into His marvelous light.* **1 Peter 2:9 NAS**

Coming up on Edisto Beach, SC and having a name that was not a local name, I often wondered about my ancestors. It was not until I had served my draft time and had a job Columbia, SC that I found an area of South Carolina where the Lybrand name was a local name. There is even a street named Lybrand after a Mayor of West Columbia.

I met a distant cousin up there and he told me that the Lybrand's got a Land Grant in 1753 between Irmo, SC and Lexington, SC. Of course, neither of these towns were there at the time.

This began my search. I first went to the South Carolina Archives, located in Northeast Columbia and found the original Land Grant and survey of the land that went with the Land Grant. From there I spent about two years finding out all I could about my direct ancestors.

While living in the Columbia area I met several nice black gentlemen with the last name Lybrand. After I got to know them, they called me, 'cousin'.

In Columbia, I sold real estate for 30 years before moving back to Edisto Island. In the Columbia/Lexington area my name was a local name and therefore I was able to do well because I was not considered a New Comer.

# An Extra Story!

I love to laugh although life is hard and everything seems to go wrong when you get 83 years old like me. But when I received the next picture I laughed and said to myself, "How many people know how to catch an alligator?" In my teenage years our house was on the edge of a 500-acre Marine Forest that had many fresh water lagoons where alligators lived. I spent many, many hours exploring this wonder land.

In that forest there were large pipes under some old roads that connected some of these lagoons. Sometimes there were alligators in these old pipes. When we felt brave my brother would take a long stick and push it under the old pipe and sometimes an alligator would come out the other end. We were very aware that large gator may be in these pipes and stayed alert when doing this.

I would stand on the other end with a stick forked at one end and if a small alligator would stick his head out, I would quickly put the stick behind the head of the gator and pull the gator out, if it was less than four feet. Any larger I would tell my brother, "Let us get out of here, the gator is bigger than us!" We would drop everything and run.

Messing with alligators is not recommended. Recently a lady that lived on a neighboring island got too closed to a gator foolish trying to pet it. The gator lunged forward, grabbed her leg and pulled under water and drowned her.

If the alligator was around four five feet I would put the forked stick behind his neck and pull him out of the pipe and pull him up on the road and pull the stick back to his tail and put my hand around the stick and his tail and then carry him home. The picture on the next page shows me with my stick around a four-foot-long gator showing him to a couple of other teenagers. I don't know their names.

Another interesting thing about this picture is that I had a large old machete on my belt. When I went out into the woods, I was always ready for anything.

I had a great life as a teenager. Read my book titles: **Sam's Edisto Island Paradise** on Amazon and you will get an idea of some of the stuff that interest me as a teenager. Where our family lived had a great deal with the opportunities I had.

From time to time I will have extra material in this book just because I am an old storyteller.